MICROWAVE COOKING À La Carte

CLARE FERGUSON

MICROWAVE COOKING À La Carte

CLARE FERGUSON

GRUB STREET · LONDON

Published by
Grub Street
The Basement
10 Chivalry Rd
London SW11 1HT

ISBN 0 948817 34 8

Printed and bound in the UK
by Maclehose and Partners

This book was originally published
in 1985 as *Good Housekeeping
Gourmet Microwave Cookery*

A New Zealander by birth,
Clare Ferguson has travelled widely
throughout Britain, France, the
Mediterranean, Australasia and the
Far East, sampling local food with avid
interest and putting the research to
good use in her highly original and
personal recipes.

Immensely energetic and talented, she
is passionately interested in developing
new approaches to creative cookery
and brings great imagination to the
microwave oven.

Now established as an author,
journalist and broadcaster, this is her
third book.

C·O·N·T·E·N·T·S

*I dedicate this book to my husband, Ian,
without whose help and support it could never
have been written, and to Maurice, who
taught us to see with his eyes.*

*I also wish to thank my assistants, Lyn, Kerry
and Berit.*

F·O·R·E·W·O·R·D

Agood cook is an eternal apprentice, and the passion for creating superb food — a time-honoured occupation — knows no cultural barriers. But the real test of any specialist craft is whether it can reflect change, by selecting, using and benefiting from new discoveries, while remaining true to its own high standards. Above all it must continue to be a source of inspiration.

I am frequently asked by those who care about good cooking whether the microwave oven could diminish the cook's skills or lead to a reduction in culinary standards. Many self-styled gourmet cooks too often view the microwave oven not as the ingenious piece of kitchen equipment it really is, but as a device of doubtful usefulness, used merely to defrost food, keep ready-prepared dishes warm, or reheat them in minutes instead of hours. On the contrary, I know it to be one of the most exciting developments ever in the cookery field.

Many people who appreciate good food are concerned lest the microwave concept might be incompatible with their idea of the fine-tasting splendid dishes they have always enjoyed cooking. I can assure them that food cooked in the microwave oven retains not only a far purer, nearer-to-the-original flavour, but requires less of the liquid which can dissolve and wash away nutrients, little added fat, minimal salt and seasonings, and gives a succulence which can only come from food very quickly and freshly cooked. I must honestly agree that few foods emerge with a very crisp brown crust. But tasty golden surfaces that brown naturally and internal colours fresh as a paintbox are often preserved in a near-magical manner. Gone are the days of faded green beans and discoloured aubergine. Écrevisses stay scarlet and herbs remain freshly green. Food in its true colours!

In the course of preparing this book I therefore decided to eschew all conventional means of cooking. Each and every one of its recipes can be made in a kitchen equipped solely with a microwave oven. The oven is then made to perform as a multi-functional device: as element, as bain-marie, as steamer, as slow cooker, flash stir-frier and as a conventional oven for baking and roasting.

The number of microwave owners has rapidly increased in recent years and the trend continues upwards. In addition, new conventional cooker models now come equipped with their own inbuilt microwave oven. So unless you are determined to remain set in your culinary ways, unwilling to break with gastronomic tradition, this cookbook will demonstrate some original ways to prepare food of exceptional quality that will also meet the standards worthy of a true gourmet.

This book is not a general handbook: it is a personal collection of recipes which I have devised, researched and tested. They are offered here, re-tested and approved by the Good Housekeeping Institute, purely to exploit the exciting potential that the use of a microwave oven offers. For me, food is a constant source of delight and fascination. And that is why I have written this book.

I·N·T·R·O·D·U·C·T·I·O·N

MICROWAVES:
GETTING THE BASICS
RIGHT

The greatest care has been taken in this book with instructions on the preparation of ingredients and techniques of working — methods of cutting; the shape and dimensions of the dishes; sizes and weights of the foods; the preparation and arrangement of the food on or in its container; the need for the food to be halved, pierced, left whole, cooked covered or uncovered. All these factors greatly influence the success or failure of each recipe, for employing the correct microwave technique is of paramount importance in this sort of cooking. Mistakes can occur so very quickly and, alas, are often irreversible.

WHAT ARE MICROWAVES?

Microwave ovens transmit electrical energy by means of microwaves, which are electro-magnetic waves of very short length and high frequency. This way of disseminating energy is called radiation. Radiation can be of two types: ionising (which can be hazardous) and non-ionising (which does not damage human cells). Microwaves are of this second type and are particularly attracted to water molecules. By means of agitating (to thousands of millions of times a second) these water molecules in food, the temperature within the food itself is raised. In traditional cooking, the oven temperature is raised by transference of heat. But in microwave cooking, heat is produced essentially within the food itself, particularly by water, fat and sugar molecules.

HOW A MICROWAVE OVEN WORKS

Inside a microwave oven, electrical energy from the mains is changed from high direction voltage to indirectional voltage. This is then converted by

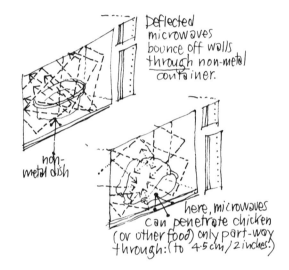

Deflected microwaves bounce off walls through non-metal container.

non-metal dish

here, microwaves can penetrate chicken (or other food) only part-way through: (to 4.5 cm / 2 inches.)

a fuse called the magnetron into electro-magnetic energy. In some cases a 'waveguide' or 'stirrer fan', set in the side or roof of the oven, concentrates the waves and bounces them in all directions off specially constructed walls and the specially sealed door and door frame. Other models have a turntable to assist in the distribution of the microwaves. This action can only take place if the safety door is shut, completing the safety seal. It can never happen if the door is even slightly ajar. If the door is accidentally opened the process automatically shuts off. Stringent official regulations check the safety of all machines permitted entry to this country.

Microwaves are *deflected* by metal; *pass through* glass, china, plastic, paper and wood; and *act upon* the molecules of the food itself.

Microwaves penetrate to a depth of 4.5 cm (about 2 inches) into the top, bottom and sides of the food so that pieces less than 9–10 cm (4 inches) thick start to cook immediately from internal heat, and not because they are surrounded by hot air or are touching a hot surface. This is why heatproof glass, china, plastic, paper and wood can be used as cooking vessels. Microwaves pass through them without the containers themselves becoming hot, unless heat from the hot food transfers itself to them. No metal cooking vessels should ever be used. Microwaves do not penetrate metal; they bounce off it and may therefore damage the magnetron. Tiny amounts of metal foil may be used, however, to protect small areas from overcooking, since they deflect the microwaves from that one place.

Browning

In order to 'brown' food in microwave ovens with no browning mechanism, heat must be 'attracted', so the food must contain high amounts of fat or sugar. Certain glazes, marinades and seasonings containing these substances may be used to help in this process.

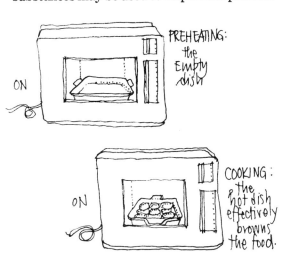

PREHEATING: the Empty dish

ON

COOKING: the hot dish effectively browns the food.

ON

Conventional cooking processes produce crisp, crusty surfaces of bread, toast and fried potatoes through surface caramelization by transferred heat. A microwave oven cannot easily perform this function. 'Browning dishes' are therefore recommended for the purpose. After preheating, these dishes can act much like a frying pan. The retained heat in their base is transferred to the surface of the food, thereby browning it, when the two come into contact. More recent microwave ovens can brown food within the cavity of the oven itself. Browning is also one of the functions incorporated into the pre-programmable controls of some kinds of microwave oven.

POWER SETTINGS AND HEAT CONTROLS

When manufacturers refer to a 700-watt oven they are referring to the oven's *power output*; its *input*, which is indicated on the back of the oven, would be double that figure.

The higher the wattage of an oven the faster the rate of cooking, thus food cooked at 700 watts on full power will cook in twice the time as food cooked at 350 watts. That said, the actual cooking performance of one 700-watt oven may vary from another with the same wattage because factors like oven cavity size affect cooking performance.

Unlike conventional ovens the various microwave ovens have yet to be standardised. A HIGH or full power setting on one oven may be 500 watts while on another model HIGH or full power is 700 watts. The vast majority of ovens sold today are either 600-, 650- or 700-watt ovens but there are many ovens still in use which have between 400 and 500 watts.

In this book HIGH refers to full power output of 700 watts, MEDIUM corresponds to 60 per cent of full power and LOW is 35 per cent of full power. If your oven power output is lower than 700 watts, allow a longer cooking time for all recipes in this book.

THE GOURMET MICROWAVE OVEN

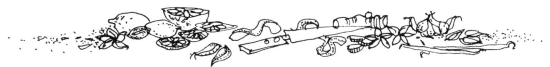

* The recipes in this book were created using a 700-watt microwave oven with stirrer fan rather than a turntable. Its dimensions were 23.5 cm (9½ in) high; 32.5 cm (13 in) wide and 42.5 cm (17 in) deep. Ovens of smaller size may require an adjustment to the amount of food which can be cooked at one time. Take this into account when considering individual recipes. Two sizes of browning dish were also frequently used to assist in the browning of certain foods.

MICROWAVE COOKING TECHNIQUES

It is important to understand and adhere to the following in order to get the best from the microwave oven.

COVERING FOOD WITH CLING FILM

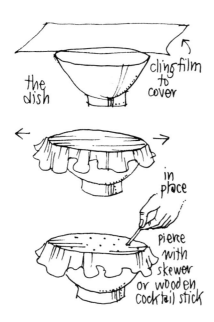

If the container and food are covered with plastic cling film (heavier grades work best) which is pierced or left slightly unsealed in one corner, the food cooks by steaming or poaching as well as by microwaves.

The cling film must ALWAYS be pierced to prevent a build up of steam and pressure. Assume that most dishes are to be cooked covered, unless otherwise stated, the exceptions being pan-fried or stir-fried dishes and roasts. If less of a steamed effect is needed, cover the food loosely with cling film, or cover only $\frac{7}{8}$ or $\frac{3}{4}$ of the surface, leaving one corner free so that it can be stirred through the opening if necessary, without the need to remove and replace the cling film.

Food can be cooked on LOW, MEDIUM or HIGH as long as these points are followed:

● If covering a dish with a lid, always remove it carefully. The build-up of heat and steam from inside and heat conduction will make the lid hot.

● When food has cooked on HIGH for a long

time, always peel off the cling film from the side furthest away from you. Thus steam does not accumulate near the face.

COVERING FOOD WITH PAPER

Use greaseproof or silicone paper when partially covering food to prevent it from becoming soggy. If the food need not be turned often, secure the paper in place with cocktail sticks.

When reheating or cooking food which should have no surface moisture (such as bread rolls), or when the splattering of fat could cause problems (with bacon, for example), cover the dish loosely with one or two sheets of absorbent kitchen paper.

WRAPPING FOODS

Foods can be completely cooked in edible leaves; *en papillote* in greaseproof or silicone paper, twisted loosely or folded beneath; in paper bags; in heavy duty plastic bags, heatproof bags, or oven bags; baskets, and so on. No metal fastenings, however, must be used. String, rubber bands or non-metallic ties will suffice to secure the bag loosely. Pierce it in several places. Since microwave cooking efficiency is slowed by an accumulation of juices, untie the bag partway through the cooking time and empty the liquid contents into a separate container, reserving for later use.

ROTATION

9 identical cups

*if this one boils first then it shows position of "hot spot."

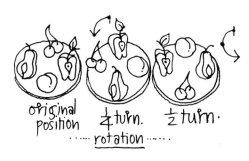

original position   ¼ turn.   ½ turn.

······ rotation ······

Many, if not most, microwave ovens have 'hot spots' which tend to overcook food in one particular area. Test for this by putting nine identical glasses or cups, with identical volumes of water, in an even pattern in the microwave oven. Microwave on HIGH, uncovered. The first water to boil is positioned on the 'hot spot'.

Food pieces can be stirred within their dish, or the dish itself can be rotated by giving it a quarter, or a half, or a three-quarters turn to ensure that even cooking is maintained.

ARRANGEMENT OF FOOD

A straight sided, ring shaped container will always give the best results, as microwave energy can enter from both sides and the top.

Straight sided round or oval dishes usually give better results than square or rectangular ones, as corners produce over cooking. Food in shallow dishes cooks quicker than in deep dishes.

If the dish is rectangular or oval, then arrange the portions alternately with denser areas towards the outside (as shown). If the height of each portion is more than 6 cm (2½ inches) then

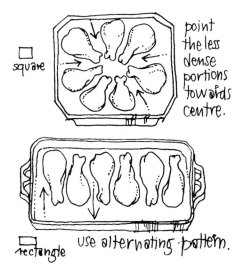

square

point the less dense portions towards centre.

rectangle   use alternating pattern.

the portions should be turned over halfway through the cooking time.

If the dish is circular or square, then point the thinner or less dense parts of the portions towards the centre (as shown). If the thickest part of each portion is higher than 6 cm (2½ inches) then the pieces must be turned over halfway through cooking time.

If using a muffin dish, rotate the whole dish a quarter turn four times during cooking.

USING A BROWNING DISH

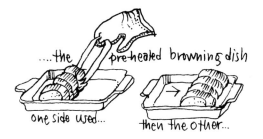

...the pre-heated browning dish

one side used...   then the other...

Follow the manufacturer's instructions regarding heating times, cleaning and treatment of the browning dishes. These dishes will become your microwave 'frying pan', but because they are not visibly hot, great care must be taken when moving them (use oven gloves) or when putting any food into the oil, butter or syrup which, added to an already hot dish, can become very hot indeed.

If browning a large joint or trussed bird, use one section of the dish to brown one side of the joint then, using tongs, turn the joint over onto the still hot 'unused' section to brown the other side.

HEAT RETENTION AND STANDING TIME

The internal temperature of many dishes continues to rise so that they 'cook' even after they are removed from the microwave oven. Allow 'standing time' for the residual heat in food to be evenly distributed. This can also 'plump up' the tissues of meats and poultry, making them easier to carve, as in traditional cookery. Absolute timings are not always indicated for this stage so use your own judgement.

Because food continues to cook after it has left the oven, it may be necessary to arrest the process sometimes. Do this by 'cooling over ice' and stand the container over a bowl of ice or iced water.

Smaller items such as pasta, for example, cool down very quickly and should be served soon after cooking.

Cover large joints of meat, while making sauce or gravy for example, in a loosely folded 'tent' of metal foil so that it does not lose heat but becomes succulent and completes its cooking cycle.

Note that jacket potatoes and similar foods can be very hot even after standing time and tenting, so beware!

MEASURING HEAT
A thermometer specially designed for the microwave is inserted deep into the central

USEFUL TIPS

All meat, poultry, game, offal and fish should be selected fresh and in prime condition.

Meat
Stewed or casseroled meat must always be covered by liquid or it may discolour. Some meat pieces may need to be pierced before cooking to hasten tenderising.

A neat, evenly symmetrical cut (such as loin, boned and rolled sirloin, pork fillet or chicken suprême) cooks well in the microwave oven as it has relatively few of the 'thick' or 'thin' areas which can cause unevenness in cooking. Larger pieces often need to be turned over halfway through cooking time. When roasting joints, use tongs to prevent the flesh being pierced and allowing juices to escape. In some recipes this is stated because it is particularly important, but assume it as a general rule unless the food is delicate, in which case it is not turned over.

Colouring
Marinating and glazing meats adds taste, colour and often tenderness to certain recipes. In most cases, however, a roast will brown if it has been in the microwave oven for 18 minutes. Once it comes out it continues to 'cook' by residual heat.

If cooked in an oven bag it is more likely to deepen in colour (use no metal ties for such bags). Soy sauce, sesame oil, honey or caramel based glazes will add surface colour to roasts, if required, without using the browning dish.

Trussing poultry
Make sure that whole birds are securely trussed to form a compact shape for even cooking. Spatchcocked birds are already flattened evenly.

Stirring
Use a wooden spoon or spatula to stir fry or stir meat and sauce mixtures. This will also avoid scratching surfaces of specially treated browning dishes or heatproof glass, plastic or ceramic dishes. Stir from the edges towards the middle always, for even results.

Use of salt
Although salty foods and cured meats (such as smoked bacon) are often not recommended for microwave cookery, I have found their limited use to be perfectly satisfactory. Use of salt should, however, be minimal and it should be dissolved in liquid quickly. Since many foods in microwave cookery retain their own 'distinctiveness', the amount of added salt becomes a matter of very personal taste. Freshly ground pepper almost always gives a savour. Use my recommendations as a guide.

portion of meat, game or poultry. It indicates internal temperature only.

Probes are now 'built-in' to many microwave ovens, and can 'hold' foods to a perfect internal temperature for set periods.

Humidity detectors are used in some microwave ovens. These show when the cling-wrapped food first emits a 'puff' of steam, indicating that it is cooked.

CONTAINERS FOR MICROWAVE COOKING

Metal containers must NEVER be used in a microwave oven. To ascertain the suitability of other types of dish, mug, plate or casserole, stand it in the microwave oven and place a glass half filled with cold water inside or beside it. If the dish remains cool and the water is hot, then the dish is 'heatproof' and suitable as 'microware'. If the dish becomes warm and the water is hot then the dish is less suitable, but usable. If the dish becomes hot and the water stays cool, then the dish is absorbing too much microwave energy and may break.

Some containers used in conventional cookery will make excellent microware dishes, once tested as safe. Speciality microwave ware such as fluted ring moulds, plastic domes, oven racks, grilling trays, plate stackers and loaf dishes are now available from large department stores and specialist microware suppliers. Together with your own tested equipment, these can make your microwave oven more adaptable, so that creating meals is more fun and less effort.

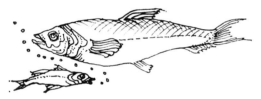

Fish
Fish cooks evenly and well in the microwave oven in even-sized portions or when rolled up and secured with wooden sticks or skewers. Another useful technique is diagonal scoring or criss-cross cutting to open out the surface of round or whole fish. (Some small fish can be turned over; others become damaged and are better left in their original position. Membranes such as fish eyes should be pierced before cooking.)

Game and offal
Game, well matured, does well in the microwave oven if cooked minimally. Offal, too, cooks well but must be halved, sliced or pierced first.

Shellfish
Live shellfish are best killed and cooked by immersing them in a large, shallow vessel of boiling water. Be accurate about volume as microwave efficiency is reduced by large amounts of water. Follow the instructions in the recipe.

Eggs
No eggs in the shell can ever be cooked in the microwave oven — they will explode. Raw, shelled eggs can only satisfactorily be cooked whole if the yolk membrane is pierced first — otherwise it too will rupture and explode. Rather than use the tip of a sharp knife I prefer to keep small, sharp wooden cocktail sticks, skewers or bamboo satay sticks to hand. With these I make several tiny holes round the edge of each yolk, without noticeable leakage (which is not only unsightly but interferes with the cooking process).

Fruit and vegetables
Fruits and vegetables chosen for cooking in the microwave should be ripe, fresh, unblemished and as even in size as possible. To distribute heat more efficiently, it is often best to slice, dice, quarter, score or halve them lengthwise. In many cases, the water that clings to them after washing is almost all that is needed to cook them. Salt added dry may cause discoloration and surface 'burn'. Follow the instructions given with individual recipes for best results. Jacket potatoes or similar vegetables, or fruit cooked whole, must be pierced several times using a skewer or fork to prevent them exploding.

MICROWAVE MAGIC

The microwave oven is excellent for:

★ Heating baby bottles at odd hours, and since many of the ovens are portable they can also be moved into a sickroom.

★ Drying herbs and flowers (between sheets of kitchen paper) and preserving their colour, texture and aroma.

★ Red wine which should have been brought to room temperature hours before. Give it a microwave 'boost' in a jug or heatproof carafe to chambré it.

★ Coffee beans. Re-roast slightly stale coffee beans on a flat plate for excellent results. Stir frequently from edges to centre.

★ Oranges, lemons and limes. If given a short burst in the microwave oven, these will give far more juice when squeezed.

★ Hard butter, stiff but creamy cheeses and rigid paté, which can all be softened by judicious use of the microwave oven on LOW bursts.

★ Chocolate, which softens and melts well in the microwave without added liquid.

★ Nuts, desiccated coconut and certain seeds (such as sesame). If stirred from sides to centre, these will brown without any added oil or fat.

★ Creamed mixtures (such as butter and sugar). They can become lighter and tastier if given a few seconds, covered, in the microwave oven.

★ Mobility. The microwave oven can be put on to a trolley and wheeled out to the barbecue, poolside or to the fund-raising party or fête to warm rolls, cook burgers and reheat ready-brewed coffees.

★ Self-timing. Once you begin to smell the food cooking, it has probably had sufficient time in the oven and is ready!

NOTES ON RECIPES AND INGREDIENTS

My selection of recipes is to some degree a matter of personal taste. It also reflects personal experience in experimenting with the microwave oven. In general I have tried to exploit its strengths and versatility. Wherever possible, I have shown through Cook's and Serving Tips and recipe introductions how to make the food just a little more special; I have also tried to emphasize how versatile some foods can be. For example, certain vegetable dishes may be served as salads, luncheons or starters. Some preserves would be excellent as desserts and sauces, and so on. By the same token, a large section on sauces, dips and glazes is included, primarily because these give the cook so many different possibilities and options for bringing out the best in their chosen dishes.

As a gourmet always prefers to seek out food in season and in the freshest condition possible, I have not advocated the use of frozen foods in these recipes. A few call for bottled or canned ingredients or condiments. This is because they offer some specific advantage of taste, quality or texture. Certain dried foods are also used, for the same reasons.

However, some Good Housekeeping microwave cooking charts have been included as a useful guide for those attempting to cook dishes or ingredients not included in this book (see page 122). When following a specific recipe from *Good Housekeeping Gourmet Microwave Cookery*, though, always time your cooking according to the instructions it gives.

For the best results, use the ingredients stipulated in the recipes. Where these are difficult to obtain, acceptable substitutes may be used. The original ingredients will, however, add that all-important 'extra' quality to the dish.

CREAM, CHEESE AND YOGURT

* My recipes include single, whipping and double creams, clotted cream, thick and soured creams. They provide, in sauces, mousses and purées, a richness and texture of particular subtlety. Imported French crème fraîche is a superb product, silky in the mouth, sourer than whipped cream yet lighter and more clean-tasting. Fromage blanc is somewhere between crème fraîche, yogurt and cheese in my view. It has a pleasant, light delicate graininess and is tremendously refreshing used in any recipe.

Many of the following cheeses are imports from Italy, France, America, Germany and Scandinavia, although good versions are now made in this country: grainy curd cheese, dryish ricotta (whey cheese), mascarpone (velvety-like cream), quark and cottage cheeses, full fat cream cheese and flavoured cheeses such as Boursin.

Plain or 'natural' yogurt now comes in a bewildering number of varieties. I tend to use the thickest strained Greek variety, which is far creamier in texture than most yogurts. For drinks, soups or to achieve a lighter effect, use a low fat variety if you must, but nothing can replace the perfection of good Greek yogurt. (I always prefer to buy plain yogurt and flavour it myself than buy prepared products, though these are becoming better and less sweet in response to public demand.)

WINES AND STOCK

* I make no excuse for using wine frequently in my cooking. I regard it, quite simply, as the best flavoured 'basic stock' imaginable for savoury dishes, sweet dishes and beverages alike. The amounts needed are often small, yet the benefits bestowed immense. Many of the specified liqueurs are available as miniatures.

Finally, a small bottle of kitchen brandy, kitchen vermouth and dry sherry, all fortified and 'good keepers', seem not too much of an extravagance to those who value good food.

Whenever possible use homemade stock from raw bones, carcasses or herbs. Not only do these give the best flavour but, when reduced, give the syrupy consistency so necessary for good sauces.

SEASONINGS

* Ready made seasonings, such as seasoned salts, herbs, smooth or coarse grained mustards, fish extracts, chilli and other pastes and sauces, honeys, fruit jellies and conserves are used with specific purpose throughout these recipes. Substitutes or omissions cannot be expected to produce the desired results.

AROMATICS

* Aromatics such as orange, lemon and lime peel, scented teas, green peppercorns, fresh root ginger, garlic cloves, cinnamon sticks, vanilla bean pods, freshly extracted seeds, berries or flower heads are often used twisted, crushed, bruised or crumbled in my recipes. These treatments help to extract the maximum aroma during the shorter cooking times, though in many cases microwave ovens tend to accentuate such flavours.

OILS AND BUTTERS

* Olive oil comes in many grades, the finest being extra virgin olive oil and then virgin olive oil. Both of these have been cold pressed (no heat applied during manufacture); they have low oleic acidity, wonderful aroma, colour and taste, and a mellow 'fruitiness'.

Locate, buy and bring back the best oil you can afford when travelling abroad or cultivate a good supplier in your area. Olive oil is best kept out of the light: cans or coloured glass bottles will protect it from the ravages of sunlight. 'Pure' olive oil, a lower grade, has been hot pressed and is perfectly good for many recipes, in blends or in dressings.

In general, seed oils such as grapeseed are good for most uses in cooking where no particular added taste is required. I often use a blend of seed oil with some distinctive-tasting nut oil.

Nut oils, such as hazelnut and walnut, though expensive and not recommended for normal cooking at high temperatures, seem to give good results in microwave cooking when used with another oil or butter, or when used to dress freshly-cooked food for use hot or cold.

Butters, too, vary in taste, colour, quality and degree of saltiness. Use the type you most prefer, although unsalted butter does give a delectable, clean taste. On the other hand, I like the vigour that many salted butters provide and use them often. Clarified butter is specified for one or two recipes and should not be confused with *ghee*, which has a very distinctive flavour. For use in the microwave oven, butter should be at room temperature.

EGGS

* Note that unless otherwise stated, size 3 or 4 eggs should be used in the following recipes.

S·T·A·R·T·E·R·S, S·O·U·P·S A·N·D S·N·A·C·K·S

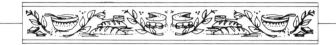

WOODCUTTERS' SALAD

I was recently served salad a little like this in a pleasant country pub in Bray, near Windsor. The previous time I had savoured such a dish was in a tiny restaurant with an open fire, on the outskirts of Barbizon in France. On both occasions I was working, which added to my pleasure: the lunch was a bonus. Somehow the name Woodcutters' Salad seems to bring back both these rural associations.

Serves 4

Dressing

30 ml (2 tbsp) oil

25 g (1 oz) rinded Polish Bozcek (or either smoked streaky bacon or Danish smoked loin) cut into 0.5 cm ($\frac{1}{4}$ inch) strips

4 lambs' kidneys, skinned, cored and quartered

5 ml (1 level tsp) Dijon mustard

1 garlic clove, skinned and crushed

30 ml (2 level tbsp) flat leaf parsley, coarsely chopped

15 ml (1 tbsp) red wine vinegar

salt and pepper to taste

Salad

1 red onion, peeled, sliced and separated into rings

1 head of chicory, broken into leaves

1 bunch watercress

$\frac{1}{2}$ red oak leaf lettuce (or other red-leaf lettuce or endive), torn into pieces

1 handful young dandelion leaves (optional)

1. Preheat a 20 cm (8 inch) browning dish on HIGH for 5 minutes.
2. Add the oil, bacon and kidneys and toss together vigorously to seal the meat. Do not allow the kidneys to stick. Microwave, uncovered, on HIGH for 2 minutes, stirring halfway through cooking time.
3. Add the mustard, garlic, red wine vinegar and seasonings to the pan, stirring quickly to blend. Then add the parsley.
4. Have the onion, chicory, watercress, lettuce and dandelion leaves ready on 4 serving dishes or in one large salad bowl.
5. Empty the still-hot contents of the pan into the salad, toss quickly and eat while the salad is warm but the vegetables still retain some crispness.

See photograph page 25.

—— SERVING TIP ——
Some firm, dark country bread is good for mopping up the juices and a robust red wine such as Pomerol, or a good Rioja, would give a pleasing balance to such a meal.

PASTA AUX TROMPETTES

'Straw and hay' pasta, to use its popular Italian name, is a mixture of plain and green finely cut noodles. With a firm and particular texture all their own, they also look delightful. In this recipe I combine them in a saffron-scented sauce flavoured with those mushrooms (dried in this case) oddly named 'death trumpets'. This rich concoction is excellent eaten alone, as a starter, light lunch, supper dish or an accompaniment to grills, roast poultry or game.

Serves 4

15 g (½ oz) dried Trompettes de la mort mushrooms
225 g (8 oz) fresh paglia e fieno tagliarini
25 g (1 oz) softened butter
50 g (2 oz) shallot, peeled and sliced
1.9 g sachet powdered saffron
15 ml (1 tbsp) dry vermouth
15 ml (1 tbsp) lemon juice
250 ml (8 fl oz) single cream

1. Put the mushrooms in a measuring jug and just cover with hot water. Leave them to stand for 15 minutes. Drain in a plastic (or muslin lined) sieve, reserving 30 ml (2 tbsp) of the strained stock.
2. In a broad, shallow heatproof dish or casserole, quickly cover the tagliarini with 1.1 litres (2 pints) of freshly boiling water. Microwave immediately, uncovered, on HIGH for 6 minutes, stirring half-way through the cooking time. Drain through a colander.
3. Put the butter, shallot, saffron and drained mushrooms in the dish, toss gently and micro-wave, uncovered, on HIGH for 1 minute.
4. Add the reserved stock, vermouth, lemon juice and cream. Stir well and microwave, uncovered, on HIGH for 1½ minutes or until the liquid is hot and thickened.
5. Add the drained tagliarini, then toss well to coat with the sauce. Microwave, uncovered, on HIGH for 1½ minutes. Serve immediately (before it cools) as a separate course followed by a red-leaved salad or as the accompaniment to another dish.

See photograph page 25.

HERB-GARNISHED FRESH TAGLIATELLE

Although little time is saved by cooking fresh pasta in the microwave oven, the use of freshly, kettle-boiled water and a broad shallow dish means less checking, no stirring and no risk of boiling over. Do not attempt to cook larger quantities than those given here. There is sufficient fresh pasta for four persons as an accompaniment (for example, with partridge) or two as a main course.

Serves 2 or 4

225 g (8 oz) fresh wholewheat tagliatelle
1 chicken or herb stock cube, crumbled
25 g (1 oz) salted butter
6–8 spring onions, trimmed and thinly sliced
45 ml (3 level tbsp) chopped fresh parsley
10 ml (2 level tsp) black poppy seeds
salt and freshly ground black pepper

1. Have the tagliatelle ready in a large, square (or rectangular) shallow heatproof dish or casserole in the microwave oven. Quickly pour on 1.1 litres (2 pints) boiling water and crumble the stock cube over the pasta.
2. Immediately microwave, uncovered, on HIGH for 5 minutes. Drain well in a colander.
3. To the same heatproof dish, add the butter, spring onions, parsley, poppy seeds and drained tagliatelle. Microwave, uncovered, on HIGH for 1 minute, then toss well. Season with salt and freshly ground black pepper. Serve.

--- COOK'S TIP ---

For best results use good quality fresh pasta which has been rolled out particularly thinly. This adds to the dish's charm and also helps it to cook evenly. Do not be tempted to substitute dried pasta.

LEMONY KIPPER PÂTÉ

Serve scoops of this pâté in scallop or other shells, accompanied by crusty brown bread, wholewheat melba toast or crackers. Briefly cooking the shallot and lemon rind in the same bowl in which the pâté is to be made saves time and effort and gives an excellent flavour. Try other variations too, using smoked trout or smoked mackerel.

Serves 4

| 1 lemon rind, finely shredded |
| 2 shallots, skinned and chopped |
| 50 g (2 oz) unsalted butter |
| 200 g (7 oz) kipper fillets, skinned |
| 85 g (3½ oz) cream cheese |
| 1.25 ml (¼ tsp) ground bay leaves |
| freshly ground black pepper |
| juice of 1 lemon |

1. Put the lemon rind, shallots and butter in a medium, deep heatproof bowl. Cover with cling film and microwave on HIGH for 1 minute until the shallots are tender and the butter has melted.
2. Flake the kipper and add to the bowl with the cream cheese, bay and pepper. Beat well with an electric or rotary beater or fork until roughly blended but not absolutely smooth.
3. Stir in the lemon juice and serve chilled.

SAVOURY YELLOW PEPPER SORBET

Golden-coloured, icy cold, yet hot with the bite of garlic and chilli, this paradoxical ice is just the thing to awaken the appetite and startle the taste buds. See how discerning your diners are: how many of them can guess what the sorbet contains?

Serves 4–6

| 4 medium yellow peppers |
| 1 clove garlic, skinned and crushed |
| ½ small fresh red chilli, seeded and sliced |
| 30 ml (2 level tbsp) caster sugar |
| 90 ml (6 tbsp) medium sweet white wine |
| 2 egg whites |
| pinch of salt |

Garnish

| sprigs of coriander or chervil |

1. Slice each pepper crosswise to remove a small lid of stem and flesh. Set these lids aside. Discard the seeds and membranes, then slice the flesh into thin strips.
2. Put the pepper strips, garlic and chilli into a medium heatproof bowl. Cover with cling film and microwave on HIGH for 2 minutes.
3. Stir in the sugar and wine, then purée this mixture using a food processor or blender. Cool over ice.
4. Whisk the egg whites with salt until stiff peaks form, then fold into the cooled pepper purée. Turn into a shallow, freezeproof plastic container, cover, seal and fast freeze for 2 hours or until frozen to a slush. Crush using a food processor or electric beater.
5. Cover the container and seal again, freezing until firm (about 1½ hours).
6. 'Ripen', using the microwave for 20–30 seconds on HIGH, covered.
7. Stir the mixture until it becomes crumbly. Serve scoops on to chilled plates garnished with the reserved lids and sprigs of coriander or chervil.

───── COOK'S TIP ─────
Red peppers can be used in place of the yellow variety, if wished.

HOT MUSTARD PISTACHIO AND HERB BREAD

Flamboyance and flavour are achieved by blending garlic butter with one or two unusual ingredients. This loaf is equally good for picnics or as the prelude to a cold soup or salad meal.

Serves 4–6

1 small baguette (or similar French loaf)

50 g (2 oz) butter

2 garlic cloves, skinned and crushed

30 ml (2 level tbsp) green herb mustard

30 ml (2 level tbsp) chopped fresh mixed herbs

25 g (1 oz) shelled, salted pistachio nuts, finely chopped

1. Slash the bread at 2.5 cm (1 inch) intervals almost through to the base.
2. If the butter is cold, put it in a heatproof bowl and microwave on LOW for 30 seconds or until it is soft enough to spread easily.
3. Beat the remaining ingredients into the butter and spread one side of each slice with this mixture.
4. Wrap the bread completely in greaseproof paper and microwave on HIGH for 1½ minutes or until hot.
5. Unwrap and serve hot. If the garlic bread is not to be eaten at once, leave it wrapped and cover with foil to conserve heat.

HIGHLAND FONDUE GLENFIDDICH

This mild and mellow hot fondue is made in the same bowl from which it is then served. Oatmeal and whisky lend a certain earthy charm. Note that the varying cooking levels are important for a smoothly blended texture. A wee dram of Glenfiddich would never go amiss at the same time.

Serves 4–6

100 g (4 oz) Caboc (Scottish creamy oatmeal covered cheese)

50 g (2 oz) mature cheddar, coarsely grated

30 ml (2 level tbsp) plain flour

200 ml ($\frac{1}{3}$ pint) milk

30–45 ml (2–3 tbsp) Glenfiddich or other malt whisky

1. Slice the Caboc cheese into a heatproof serving bowl, about 1.1 litre (2 pint) in volume. Microwave, uncovered, on LOW for 1 minute to soften.
2. Toss the grated cheddar in the flour and add. Stir in the milk.
3. Loosely cover with cling film and microwave on MEDIUM for 3 minutes, stirring the fondue halfway through cooking time.
4. Microwave, loosely covered, on HIGH for 1 minute longer. Leave to stand and cool, uncovered. Stir in the whisky.

——— SERVING TIP ———
Serve warm or cool with black bread, broken oatcakes and crisp sticks of celery for dipping.

GOURMET CHICKEN STOCK

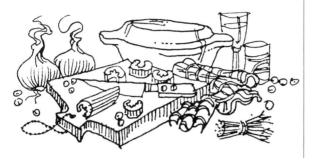

A raw chicken carcass cooked in the microwave oven makes a far tastier soup than beef or veal bones. The resulting liquid can be used in most recipes which require good light stock, and is also excellent used hot with added garnish as a soup. It may also be clarified and served chilled as it sets naturally in a delicate jellied state — so superior to the artificially set variety.

When reduced by rapid boiling, this stock becomes a strong flavoured chicken 'essence' or glaze, giving distinction to any sauce. Add a swirl of soured cream and some caviar to the jellied chicken stock for special celebrations, and a sprig of fresh tarragon. If the stock is to be kept for a few days then cover, refrigerate and re-boil it every day to prevent spoilage.

Serves 3–4 or 900 ml (1½ pints)

25 g (1 oz) butter
1 medium onion, skinned and roughly chopped
1 celery stalk, chopped
1 medium carrot, sliced
2 fresh bay leaves, crushed
8 fresh sage leaves
small bunch of fresh thyme
50 g (2 oz) bunch fresh parsley stalks
1 medium chicken carcass with giblets, both chopped
5 ml (1 level tsp) salt
5 ml (1 level tsp) black pepper corns, lightly crushed
900 ml (1½ pints) water
300 ml (½ pint) Chablis, Vouvray or dry vermouth

1. In a large heatproof mixing bowl or casserole, place the butter, onion, celery, carrot and bay leaves. Cover with cling film and microwave on HIGH for 2 minutes.
2. Add all the other ingredients and pour over them the water and wine or vermouth. Cover with a lid or loosely cover with cling film. Microwave on HIGH for about 6 minutes or until boiling, and then on MEDIUM for 40 minutes. Stir halfway through cooking time. Taste carefully, adding salt as necessary.
3. Strain the stock, discarding the solids. Taste and adjust the seasonings again once the stock has cooled. Remove the surface fat if wished.
4. Use the stock plain or garnished, or refrigerate for use later. Clarify if wished.

CHICKEN AND COURGETTE SOUP

Using your own freshly-prepared chicken stock makes a homely soup more than usually tasty. Good for brunch, lunch or supper and similar to vichyssoise (but using courgettes in place of leeks), this soup will please young, old or even jaded palates.

Serves 4

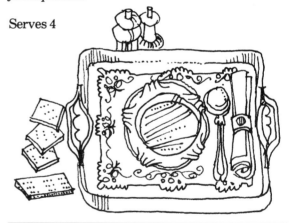

25 g (1 oz) butter
1 medium onion, skinned and chopped
175 g (6 oz) potato, cut into 1.5 cm (½ inch) cubes
450 g (1 lb) courgettes, sliced or cubed
30 ml (2 level tbsp) chopped fresh parsley
900 ml (1½ pints) homemade chicken stock (see previous recipe)
salt and freshly ground black pepper
1.25 ml (¼ tsp) freshly grated nutmeg

1. Put the butter, onion and potato cubes into a large, deep, heatproof soup tureen or casserole. Cover and microwave on HIGH for 2 minutes, stirring twice.
2. Add the courgettes and parsley and microwave on HIGH, covered, for 1 minute more.
3. Pour in the homemade chicken stock, cover with a lid and microwave on HIGH for 12 minutes, stirring 3 times.
4. Reduce the cooked solids to a purée using a food processor, blender or sieve. Season well with salt, pepper and nutmeg. Pour back into the soup tureen or casserole and serve hot with crispbreads or crackers.

GOLDEN GOURMET STOCK

Although, in microwave cookery, beef and veal bones yield a less rich broth than chicken, this meat stock is useful as a basis for many soups, sauces, fricassees, stews and casseroles – in fact any recipe that calls for a good stock. If it is to be stored over any period, then cover, refrigerate it and reboil it every day to prevent spoilage. Unlike the chicken stock it does not form jelly on cooling.

Serves 3–4

30 ml (2 tbsp) corn or soy bean oil
225 g (8 oz) beef shin, cubed
450 g (1 lb) veal bones
800 ml (1⅓ pint) water
2 medium carrots, quartered
1 medium onion, halved and unskinned
2 cloves
2 celery stalks, quartered
1 fresh bay leaf, crushed
2 fresh thyme sprigs
6–8 fresh parsley stalks
8 allspice berries, crushed
600 ml (1 pint) dry white wine or cider

1. Preheat a 25 cm (10 inch) browning dish on HIGH for 3½–4 minutes (or according to the manufacturer's instructions).

2. Add the oil, meat and bones, stir once, and then microwave, uncovered, on HIGH for 3 minutes, stirring halfway through cooking time.
3. Remove the solids from the browning dish and set them aside. Pour just 200 ml (⅓ pint) water into the dish, stirring well to dislodge all the fragments from the base of the pan.
4. Add the carrots, onion halves (each stuck with one clove) and celery. Cover with a lid and microwave on HIGH for 2 minutes.
5. Add the bay leaves, thyme, parsley stalks and allspice berries. Return the reserved browned meat and bones to the pan.
6. Pour over the remaining 600 ml (1 pint) water and the white wine or cider. Microwave, covered, with a lid, on HIGH for 45 minutes or until the stock is well flavoured.
7. Strain the stock, discarding all solids, and refrigerate. (Use the beef for potted meat spread if wished, chopping it and adding butter, spices, garlic and herbs.)
8. Taste and adjust the seasonings once the stock has cooled. Remove surface fat if wished by trailing kitchen paper across the surface. Use this stock as a basis for sauces, gravies, soups or in any recipe requiring non-poultry stock.

—— COOK'S TIP ——
Add chopped fresh herbs to the hot stock if using as a soup, and fine noodles or rice for added interest.

HOT AND SOUR GINGER SOUP

Homemade stock helps to make soups like this truly sophisticated in flavour. It's good, so I'm told, as a restorative after a long evening's carousing, which is always nice to know!

Serves 4

900 ml (1½ pints) homemade hot chicken stock (see page 20)

5 ml (1 tsp) rich soy sauce

15 g (½ oz) green ginger root, coarsely grated

30 ml (2 tbsp) syrup from preserved ginger

15 ml (1 tbsp) sherry vinegar or chilli vinegar

30 ml (2 tbsp) dry sherry or rice wine

75 g (3 oz) soy bean sprouts, cleaned

75 g (3 oz) cos lettuce or pak choy, finely shredded

1. Put all the ingredients except the soy bean sprouts and lettuce into a heatproof serving bowl. Microwave, uncovered, on HIGH for 4 minutes or until very hot.
2. Add the bean sprouts and lettuce. Cover and microwave on HIGH for a further 1 minute. Serve as a pleasant first course, lunch or supper dish.

See photograph page 25

————— **COOK'S TIP** —————
To make the soup more substantial, add some broken buckwheat noodles, dried seaweed shreds or tiny, star-shaped pasta and cook until tender. Vegetarians could use a really good vegetable broth in place of the chicken stock.

POACHED EGGS GOURMET

Poached eggs, with a little loving care and attention, become pure gourmet material whether for lunch, brunch, breakfast or supper. Serve them with one of the following sauces, and with toasted muffins for added appeal.

The first two sauces are effortlessly quick and cook at the same time as the eggs but in separate containers, which simplifies serving. The other recipes — Oeufs Paloise; Oeufs Andalouse; Oeufs Henri IV — are based on classic 19th-century culinary tradition and are perhaps suitable for more audacious entertaining. On such occasions, despite the purists who claim that eggs spoil good wine, a glass of chilled dry Vouvray complements them perfectly.

Serves 2

pinch salt

30 ml (2 tbsp) warm water

2 eggs, size 2 (at room temperature)

Gentleman's Sauce
(A delicately fish-flavoured cream)

45 ml (3 tbsp) double cream

1.25 ml (¼ tsp) Patum Peperium (anchovy relish)

5 ml (1 tsp) lemon juice

freshly ground white pepper

Garnish

2 fresh herb sprigs (parsley, tarragon or chervil)

Bedlington Sauce
(A suave and pretty sauce invented by a friend from the town of the same name)

45 ml (3 tbsp) double cream

1 pinch turmeric powder

5 ml (1 tsp) lemon juice

salt and freshly ground white pepper

Garnish

2 fresh herb sprigs (parsley, tarragon or chervil)

1. Stir the salt into the water and dissolve. Pour 2 tablespoons of salted water into 2 small 150 ml

($\frac{1}{4}$ pint) heatproof ramekins or pots. Microwave on HIGH, uncovered, for 30 seconds to heat the water.
2. Carefully break one egg into each ramekin and prick each yolk twice, using a cocktail stick.
3. Put the ingredients of the chosen sauce into a third ramekin.
4. Arrange the 3 dishes in the oven in a triangle formation equidistant from the centre. Cover each with greaseproof paper and microwave on MEDIUM for 2 minutes. Halfway through cooking time, stir the sauce to blend the ingredients thoroughly.
5. Allow the eggs to stand for 30 seconds before draining and serving with a trickle of sauce and herb garnish.

Variations

Oeufs Paloise
Cook the eggs as above, then spoon over some ready-prepared Sauce Béarnaise (page 79) to which has been added 3–4 tablespoons of freshly chopped mint.

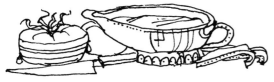

Oeufs Andalouse
Cook the eggs as above. In a ramekin, cook 2 thick slices of tomato. Place each drained egg on a hot tomato slice and spoon on some ready-prepared Pimento Coulis (page 77).

Oeufs Henri IV
Brush 2 prepared flat mushrooms with 2 teaspoons of melted butter. Cook these in a shallow heatproof dish as the eggs are poaching. Place the drained eggs on a cooked mushroom, gill side upwards, and spoon over some ready-prepared Sauce Béarnaise (page 79).

MUFFIN CUP EGG AND BACON BRUNCH

Fried eggs on a plate (those oeufs miroir *so beloved of Montparnasse and Saint Germain cafés) I have tried, without absolute success, to cook in a microwave oven. The yolk, alas, invariably sets too hard while the white remains barely cooked.*

My eventual solution was to cook the egg in the hollowed-out base of a buttered wholemeal muffin, an epicurean solution if ever there was one! The bread case warms beautifully; the white cooks faster because of the buttered surface; and the yolk, less exposed, sets gently to perfection. To complete the brunch, thinly cut bacon is cooked on the same plate at the same time.

These portions are best cooked and served one at a time as the cooking time is so brief. However, the first egg will continue to cook as it stands, so the person who prefers the softer eggs should be served last. Serve with chilled orange juice, and additional chilled champagne if a celebration is in order.

Serves 2

2 wholemeal muffins
10 ml (2 level tsp) butter
4 rashers back bacon (smoked), thinly cut
2 eggs (at room temperature)
salt and freshly ground black pepper

1. Thinly slice the lids of the muffins almost to the far edge, leaving a 'hinge', and fold open. Scoop out and discard the central crumbs of the muffins, leaving the bread walls intact.
2. Butter each cavity with a teaspoonful of butter. Using kitchen scissors, remove the rind from the bacon and slash the rashers at intervals.
3. Carefully break an egg into each muffin and prick each yolk twice, using a wooden cocktail stick. Put the muffin on one side of a heatproof serving plate and the bacon slices on the other. Cover them with folded absorbent kitchen paper.
4. Microwave on HIGH for 1 minute and 15 seconds.
5. Cover the plate with a napkin or tented foil and leave it to stand while the next portion is cooked.
6. Season the eggs with salt and pepper and serve hot.

BUTTERED EGGS WITH ASPARAGUS

The tender, thin stalks of asparagus known as sprue are used in this brunch or supper recipe. If thick-stemmed asparagus is used in its place, the stems should be halved or even quartered lengthwise, or sliced diagonally for maximum tenderness.

Serve this dish with hot toast or warm rolls.

Serves 4

225 g (8 oz) sprue (thin green asparagus stalks)
75 ml (5 tbsp) salted water
100 g (4 oz) butter (at room temperature)
6 eggs
15 ml (1 level tbsp) chives, snipped
15 ml (1 level tbsp) parsley, chopped

1. Cut the sprue into 5 cm (2 inch) lengths. Add it to the salted water in a shallow microware dish, cover with a lid, and microwave on HIGH for 5–6 minutes. Stir once halfway through cooking time. Transfer the asparagus and its cooking water to a separate dish and keep covered.
2. Put just 50 g (2 oz) of the butter in a shallow dish and microwave, uncovered, on HIGH for 30 seconds or until the butter melts.
3. Lightly beat the eggs with a fork and pour into the dish. Microwave, uncovered, on HIGH for 3 minutes, stirring from the edges to centre once a minute.
4. At the end of the cooking time, stir in the herbs with the remaining 50 g (2 oz) butter.
5. Drain the asparagus and arrange in a nest on a heated serving dish. Pile the buttered eggs in the centre and serve hot.

TOMATO AND EGG STIR FRY

This super-quick snack or meal, served with a warm roll, is best made in individual portions. Add onions and herbs of choice, depending on the season, to produce a dish that is light and quite delicious!

Serves 1

15 ml (1 level tbsp) butter
1 tomato, chopped into 16 pieces
5 ml (1 level tsp) chopped onion, spring onions or chives
2 eggs (at room temperature)
5 ml (1 level tsp) chopped fresh parsley, thyme, marjoram or basil
salt and freshly ground black pepper
1 bread roll

1. Put the butter, tomato and onion into a small, shallow-sided, heatproof serving dish and microwave on HIGH for 2 minutes, loosely covered with cling film.
2. Stir gently, pushing towards the edges of the dish. Break in the eggs and stir quickly with a fork until the yolk and white are bubbly and well mixed. Microwave, uncovered, on HIGH for 2 minutes.
3. Gently stir the mixture from outside towards the centre. Microwave on HIGH, uncovered, for a further $1\frac{1}{4}$–$1\frac{1}{2}$ minutes, stirring once from edges to centre.
4. Sprinkle with fresh green herbs and season to taste. Serve with a hot bread roll.

——— SERVING TIP ———
To serve the roll warm, wrap it lightly in absorbent kitchen paper and microwave on HIGH for 5 seconds.

Top: Hot and Sour Ginger Soup (page 22).
Left: Colourful serving of Woodcutters' Salad (page 16).
Right: Pasta aux Trompettes (page 17).
Overleaf, left: Salmon and Écrevisse with Castle Rock Sauce (page 38);
right: Berit's Mackerel Mousse with salmon 'caviar' (page 36)

Striped Trout Matisse (page 33).

CROQUES MADEMOISELLES

These two innovative versions of a French-style toasted cheese sandwich have tremendous charm, pleasing all age groups. They are the perfect snack at any time of the day or night, and the addition of fruit or fresh herbs to the melting cheese and meat seems to make them wonderfully digestible. Allow one of each flavour for every helping and serve with chilled lager or a glass of dry white wine or, for children, a chilled milk-shake.

Serves 4

---

16 thin slices white bread

40 g (1½ oz) butter

4 thin slices, 50 g (2 oz) Gruyère cheese

1 kiwi fruit, skinned and cut into 8 slices

4 thin slices Parma or Bayonne (cured) ham

50g (2 oz) mozzarella cheese, thinly sliced

8 small or 4 large fresh basil leaves

4 thin slices cooked tongue

75 ml (5 tbsp) olive oil

---

1. Butter 16 slices of bread.
2. Take 4 slices and cover with a layer of Gruyère. Add a layer of kiwi fruit (2 slices) and another of ham, then close each sandwich with a second slice of buttered bread.
3. Take 4 more buttered bread slices and cover with mozzarella. Add a layer of basil leaves and another of tongue. Close the sandwiches with the remaining buttered slices.
4. Press each sandwich down firmly and cut it into a circle using a 7.5 cm (3 inch) plain cutter.
5. Preheat a large browning dish for 3½–4 minutes, or according to the manufacturer's instructions. Quickly add 30 ml (2 level tbsp) of the olive oil (tilting pan to coat the whole surface) and add 4 of the sandwiches while the pan is very hot.
6. Microwave, uncovered, on HIGH for 30 seconds, remove the sandwiches and add another 15 ml (1 level tbsp) of olive oil. Replace the sandwiches, uncooked side down, and microwave on HIGH for 30 seconds.
7. Remove the sandwiches, put on kitchen paper, cover with tented foil and keep warm.
8. Repeat steps 5, 6 and 7 for the remaining 4 sandwiches, adding the rest of the oil as necessary.

TWICE BAKED CREAMY POTATOES

There are some instances when microwave cookery becomes an absolute bonus: not only does the food cook miraculously quickly, but the taste and finished effect seem disproportionately better than the effort expended in the making. These stuffed potatoes have only one fault: they retain so much heat that one's eagerness to eat them can result in a very burned mouth! But they're wonderful food for midnight suppers.

Be sure to prick the potato skins before cooking – or else they'll explode.

Serves 4

---

4 medium sized old potatoes, about 150–175g (5–6 oz) each

15 ml (1 level tbsp) chopped fresh parsley

50 g (2 oz) onion, skinned and coarsely grated

50 g (2 oz) tomato, chopped

100 g (4 oz) garlic-flavoured salami or spiced sausage, thinly sliced and chopped

50 g (2 oz) cheddar cheese, grated

---

1. Prick the potatoes all over with a fork. Place around the edge of a heatproof plate covered with a double thickness of absorbent kitchen paper and microwave on HIGH for 10 minutes or until tender, turning the potatoes after 5 minutes.
2. Cut lids from each potato and put aside. Scoop out the flesh and mix with the parsley, onion, tomato and spiced sausages. Spoon back into the shells and top with grated cheese.
3. Replace the lids and return the potatoes to the microwave oven. Place on absorbent kitchen paper and microwave on HIGH for 2 minutes. Serve hot (but eat with caution, as the potatoes continue cooking for some minutes and retain their heat!)

LAYERED CHICKEN LIVER TERRINES

These tasty little terrines are best made the day before they are to be eaten, as their flavour then fully develops. When sliced, they reveal their layers. Serve with crisp salad vegetables.

Serves 6

225 g (8 oz) or 12 chicken livers
200 g (7 oz) fresh white bread, cubed
150 ml ($\frac{1}{4}$ pint) milk
30 ml (2 tbsp) olive oil
45 ml (3 level tbsp) finely chopped onion
45 ml (3 level tbsp) chopped fresh parsley
2.5 ml ($\frac{1}{2}$ level tsp) chopped fresh thyme
1 egg yolk
15 ml (1 tbsp) brandy
salt and freshly ground black pepper
6 stoned, pre-soaked prunes
50 g (2 oz) roasted almonds

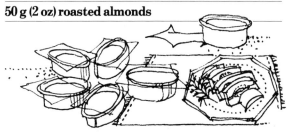

1. Clean, halve and trim the livers. Soak the bread cubes in the milk.
2. Preheat a 25 cm (10 inch) browning dish on HIGH for 3$\frac{1}{2}$–4 minutes (or according to the manufacturer's instructions). Pour in the oil and quickly add the chicken livers, stirring. Add the onion and cover with a lid. Microwave on HIGH for 2 minutes.
3. Remove the chicken livers and onion and, using a food processor, blender or mincer, finely chop them together with the drained bread cubes. Add the parsley, thyme, egg yolk, brandy and seasoning and mix well.
4. Stuff each prune with one roasted almond and coarsely chop the remaining almonds.
5. Lightly grease 6 small heatproof terrines and base line with baking parchment. Half fill each terrine with the pâté mixture and cover with a stuffed prune and a layer of chopped almonds. Cover with the remaining pâté mixture, pressing down firmly.

6. Space the terrines evenly in a circle in the microwave oven. Cover loosely with more baking parchment and microwave on HIGH for 10 minutes, re-arranging the terrines halfway through cooking.
7. Keep covered until cool, and chill before turning out. Remove the parchment before serving.

HACHIS DE VEAU AU GRUYÈRE

Educate the palate of would-be teenage gourmands by showing them how to make and cook simple but tasty burgers at home.

Serves 4

100 g (4 oz) rye bread, crumbled
30 ml (2 tbsp) single cream
450 g (1 lb) fillet of veal, finely minced
2.5 ml ($\frac{1}{2}$ level tsp) salt
5 ml (1 level tsp) dried oregano
45 ml (3 tbsp) olive oil
100 g (4 oz) Gruyère cheese, sliced into 16 strips
freshly ground black pepper
60 ml (4 tbsp) dry white wine or cider

1. Put the breadcrumbs and cream into a food processor or bowl and mix until smooth. Add the minced veal, salt and oregano and process or mix briefly until smoothly blended.
2. Divide the mixture into 4. Shape into compact balls and flatten each between the palms to make a 2 cm ($\frac{3}{4}$ inch) thick burger.
3. Preheat a large 25 cm (10 inch) round browning dish for 5–6 minutes. Quickly add the olive oil and 4 burgers, evenly spaced, and microwave on HIGH, uncovered, for 2 minutes.
4. Use a fish slice or spatula to turn the burgers over and microwave on HIGH for a further 1 minute.
5. Cover each burger with 4 parallel strips of cheese and grind black pepper over the top. Spoon the wine into the pan and microwave for a final 2 minutes.
6. Serve each burger with a little unthickened sauce.

F·I·S·H AND S·E·A·F·O·O·D

PLAICE AND PARMA ROULADES WITH VINE LEAVES

Although delicate egg yolk sauces are usually cooked slowly, in this recipe the sauce cooks quickly and easily on high power. Because freshly-picked young and tender vine leaves are not always available, I would suggest using spinach or dandelion leaves, though the effect and taste will not be quite the same.

Serves 4

four 100 g (4 oz) fillets of plaice, skinned

65 g (2½ oz) or 4 thin slices of Parma or other cured ham

30 ml (2 level tbsp) Niersteiner or other similar German wine

15 g (½ oz) butter

8 fresh young vine leaves

Sauce

1 egg yolk

30 ml (2 level tbsp) crème fraîche

salt and pepper

1. Cut each plaice fillet in half lengthways and place on a board, skinned side up.
2. Lay half a slice of ham on each halved fillet and roll up from the tail towards the head end. Push a wooden cocktail stick through each end to secure it firmly.
3. Repeat the process for the remaining roulades.
4. Space the fish evenly around the edge of a shallow 20 cm (8 inch) microwave plate or dish. Sprinkle with wine and dot with butter. Cover each roulade with pierced young vine leaves.
5. Cover the dish with a lid or cling film and microwave on HIGH for 5 minutes.
6. To make the sauce, blend the egg yolk with the crème fraîche in a sauce jug or small bowl. Stir in the juices from the fish.
7. Microwave, uncovered, on HIGH for 1 minute, stirring three times as the mixture thickens. Season to taste.
8. Remove the cocktail sticks and serve the fish with the sauce accompanied by baby potatoes and green beans.

MONKFISH KEBABS WITH CORAL ISLAND SAUCE

It both shocked and delighted me to discover that shady restaurateurs and caterers sometimes substitute the inexpensive monkfish for crayfish, or even lobster, in dishes where the appearance is somewhat disguised. The compactness of monkfish, and its delicious, clean, sweet taste are reminiscent of both: diners are at least fooled by a worthy imposter! But the monkfish looks such an odd creature, with a huge head, that it is usually presented on the fishmonger's slab in the form of skinned tails, pinkish-white. These make perfect kebabs, and the taste of coconut cream in the pale pink sauce reminds me of the coral islands of the Pacific.

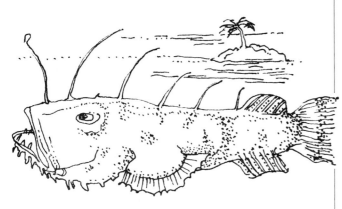

Serves 4

800 g (1¾ lb) monkfish tail

8 rashers smoked back bacon, rinded

5 ml (1 tsp) fruity olive oil

freshly ground white pepper

Sauce

175 ml (6 fl oz) Muscadet or similar dry white wine

10 ml (2 level tsp) cornflour

5 ml (1 level tsp) tomato concentrate

40 g (1½ oz) creamed coconut, chopped

15 ml (1 level tbsp) chopped fresh parsley

salt to taste

Garnish (optional)

1 fresh tomato

1. Remove the central bone from the monkfish tail by severing the flesh from each side to give 2 fillets.
2. Halve each fillet lengthwise and cut each section into 14 bite-sized chunks to give a total of 28 pieces (7 for each kebab).
3. Halve the bacon rashers crosswise to give 16 pieces.
4. Wrap each bacon piece around one chunk of monkfish. Thread the bacon-wrapped monkfish pieces alternately with the remaining unwrapped fish chunks on to 4 dried fennel stalks, or wooden or bamboo skewers, starting and ending with a bacon-wrapped piece.
5. Evenly space the kebabs around the edges of a large heatproof plate or shallow dish. Brush with olive oil and sprinkle with freshly ground pepper. Cover loosely with cling film and microwave on HIGH for 8–9 minutes, giving the dish a quarter turn halfway through the cooking time. The bacon should be cooked and the fish white and firm.
6. Remove the kebabs and wrap them in foil to keep warm while making the sauce. Pour off the fish and bacon juices into a heatproof measuring jug.
7. Make up the quantity of cooking juices to 300 ml (½ pint) with white wine. Mix together the cornflour and tomato concentrate and add this to the liquid with small pieces of the creamed coconut. Microwave, uncovered, on HIGH for 2 minutes, stirring vigorously to distribute the ingredients halfway through the cooking time, until the sauce is hot and thickened.
8. Stir freshly chopped parsley into the hot sauce and season to taste.
9. Serve one kebab for each person on a pool of sauce garnished with tomato if wished.

STRIPED TROUT MATISSE

Looking like a Matisse still life, these decorative fillets of pale pink trout are wrapped with strips of deeper pink smoked fish. Borders of fresh green herbs lie between each stripe. The taste is perfect too.

Serves 4

two 350 g (12 oz) fresh rainbow or brown trout, cleaned

Stock

30 ml (2 tbsp) good Chablis or Muscadet

30 ml (2 tbsp) water

1 shallot, peeled and finely chopped

salt and freshly ground black pepper

100 g (4 oz) smoked trout (or smoked salmon), thinly sliced

30 ml (2 tbsp) fresh dill sprigs

15 ml (1 level tbsp) butter

1. Fillet both fresh fish carefully to give 4 fillets. Set them aside and place the heads, bones and fins in a medium heatproof bowl with the wine, water and shallot. Season and microwave, covered, on HIGH for 2 minutes to extract a concentrated fish stock. Strain off this stock and reserve. There should be about 45 ml (3 tbsp) volume.
2. Cut the smoked fish into 2.5 cm (1 inch) wide strips and loosely wrap in diagonal 'stripes' at intervals along each fillet so that the ends of the strips are hidden beneath the underside (skin side) of each fillet.
3. Dot the tiny dill sprigs in lines between each 'stripe'. Arrange the fillets head to tail in a large flat dish. Pour the strained stock over the fish and cover with cling film. Microwave on HIGH for 4 minutes.
4. Serve carefully with some of the unthickened sauce poured over each fillet.

See photograph page 28

RED MULLET EL DORADO

Really fresh red mullet smell deliciously of the sea and should be a brilliant pinky red, with firm convex eyes and two pliable barbels or whiskers. Although many afficionados cook the fish ungutted, I prefer to cook it already gutted, served on this golden sauce.

Serves 4

4 red mullet, gutted and scaled, about 250 g (9 oz) each

60 ml (4 tbsp) fresh coriander

juice of 1 lemon

30 ml (2 tbsp) fruity olive oil

freshly ground black pepper

1 medium onion, skinned and sliced

Sauce

Saffron Cream Sauce (see page 79)

1. Stuff the gut cavity of each fish with equal portions of coriander. Slash each fish crosswise, 6 times on both sides, to give a lattice effect. Arrange the fish, evenly spaced, on a square or rectangular heatproof dish.
2. Sprinkle the lemon juice, oil, pepper and onion over the fish, cover loosely with cling film and leave to marinate for 15 minutes.
3. Microwave on HIGH for 9 minutes or until the flesh is pearly white and firm to the touch.
4. Carefully pour or spoon off the hot fish juices into a separate bowl. Use as the stock described in Saffron Cream Sauce (page 79).
5. Keep the fish hot until the sauce is ready to serve. Present each fish in a pool of golden sauce.

———— COOK'S TIP ————
The mullet livers are delicious and should be retained and cooked with the fish.

GREY MULLET WITH CURRIED MELON SAUCE

Grey mullet is splendid cooked and served whole. It is a fish that can be adapted to full-bodied garlicky treatments, or to more subtle fruit and herb accompaniments, as in this recipe. Here a stuffing of melon and a delicately spiced hot melon sauce are served with it.

Serves 4–6

1.1–1.4 kg (2½–3 lb) whole grey mullet, scaled and gutted

---

3 fresh bay leaves, halved lengthwise

---

1 ripe Galia melon, 700 g (1½ lb)

---

freshly ground black pepper

---

30 ml (2 tbsp) fruity olive oil

2.5 ml (½ level tsp) curry paste

---

60 ml (4 level tbsp) chopped fresh fennel sprigs

---

salt to taste

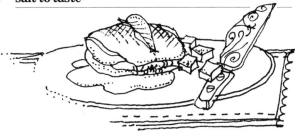

1. Put the prepared grey mullet into a large, oval heatproof dish. Make 3 diagonal slashes in the flesh and push a halved bay leaf, curved side upwards, into each slash. Turn the fish over and repeat this process on the other side. Pierce the eyes using a metal skewer.
2. Halve the melon and discard all the seeds. Remove the skin and cut the flesh into 1 cm (½ inch) cubes.
3. Grind a generous amount of black pepper over the fish and inside the gut cavity.
4. Fill the gut cavity with half the melon cubes and trickle olive oil over the fish. Cover with cling film and leave it to stand while the sauce is prepared.
5. Put the remaining melon cubes in a food processor or blender with the curry paste and process until blended. Add the fennel sprigs and salt to taste. Pour into a small heatproof sauce-boat or serving dish.
6. Microwave the cling-film covered fish on

HIGH for 11–13 minutes, or until the flesh is firm and milky-white in colour. Season with salt. Cover the fish and leave it to stand while the melon sauce cooks.
7. Microwave the sauce, uncovered, on HIGH for 1–1½ minutes or until hot. Take the fish whole to the table and serve with some melon stuffing to each portion. Allow diners to pour their sauce over the food when it is served.

SERVING TIP
This dish goes well with Basmati Rice with Herbs (page 75) or Kibbled Wheat Pilaf (page 76).

COLCHESTER OYSTERS EN BRIOCHE

Fragrant with lemon, these buttery-tender brioches make a bed for a barely-cooked oyster nestling on spinach amid a hint of Pernod. Top grade English oysters are plump, sweet and absolutely flawless. Oyster-lore must be learned from an expert fishmonger and neither of my advisors in this worthy trade, Frank nor Peter, ever blink when I request my oysters live. To the professional that is understood. For the best flavour, oysters should be opened, slid from their shells and on to the plate or into the oven within minutes.

Serves 4

---

50 g (2 oz) butter

---

finely shredded rind of 1 lemon

---

30 ml (2 tbsp) lemon juice

---

4 small (single serving) firm brioches

---

4 live Colchester or Whitstable oysters

---

75 g (3 oz) fresh spinach, roughly torn and washed

---

freshly ground black pepper

2.5 ml (½ tsp) Pernod

---

1. Cut the butter into 2.5 cm (1 inch) cubes and put in a small heatproof bowl. Microwave, uncovered, on HIGH for 20 seconds or until it

melts. Stir in the lemon rind and juice.

2. Using a grapefruit knife, cut out the centre of the brioche and remove. Discard the crumbs from the underside of each lid and reserve the lids. This should give 4 hollow brioche 'baskets' with lids and a space inside for the filling.

3. Brush the outsides and insides of each brioche and lid with the lemon butter (reserving about 5 ml [1 level tsp] for the spinach).

4. Open the oysters and free them from their shells.

5. Put the spinach on a heatproof plate and cover with cling film. Microwave on HIGH for 1 minute. Chop the hot spinach quickly, adding the reserved lemon butter, then quickly divide the mixture between the 4 brioches.

6. On each bed of spinach place 1 oyster and its juice. Grind black pepper generously over all. Replace the lids and arrange, evenly spaced, around a heatproof serving plate. Microwave on HIGH for 2 minutes. Remove the lids and sprinkle 3 drops (no more) of Pernod over each oyster. Replace the lids and serve immediately.

BUTTERFLY PRAWNS IN THEIR SHELLS

A small, homely basement restaurant in Kensington, run and staffed by Thai food specialists, inspired this dish. While you watch, the prawn shells turn from bluish-grey to deep red, indicating that they are ready to be turned. Then, shell-side down, they cook for a further minute. Seafood tasting so good yet cooked so simply is always a delight.

Serves 2 or 4

4 large raw king prawn tails
15 ml (1 tbsp) sunflower oil
15 ml (1 tbsp) sesame oil
2 cloves garlic, skinned and chopped
5 ml (1 level tsp) fresh root ginger, peeled and chopped
15 ml (1 tbsp) rice wine or dry sherry

Garnish

fresh coriander or parsley sprigs

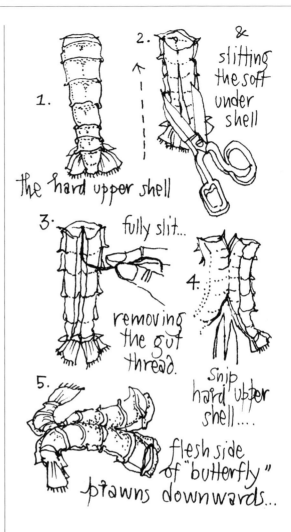

1. Preheat a 20 cm (8 inch) browning dish for 6 minutes, or according to the manufacturer's instructions.

2. Using kitchen scissors, slit the soft undershell and flesh of the prawn tails along their length almost to the end. Flatten them to expose the flesh. Find and discard the dark thread of the gut. Snip the hard upper side of the shell almost to the end and push it to open out in a butterfly effect.

3. Put the oils, garlic and ginger into the browning dish. Using tongs, position the tails flesh side down and microwave, uncovered, on HIGH for 1 minute. Again using tongs, quickly turn the prawns over and microwave, uncovered, on HIGH for a further minute.

4. Transfer the prawns to a heated serving dish and keep warm. Stir the wine or sherry into the contents of the still-hot pan, and serve the sauce immediately, poured over the prawns.

5. Garnish with sprigs of fresh coriander or parsley.

SCALLOPS WITH SNAPPER AND PRAWNS

Adventurous London fishmongers sometimes sell fish from the Seychelles, like the beautiful red snapper used with scallops and prawns in this recipe. But if this fish is unavailable then other snapper or bream varieties should be used instead. Combined with scallops, prawns and coconut shreds, the taste becomes most exotic indeed: a veritable seafood rendezvous! In order to include the colourful snapper skin ask your fishmonger to scale the fish for you, otherwise your kitchen will be awash with the tough 1 cm (½ inch) scales as you remove them. I always buy prawns in their shells and peel them myself for the best results, and the debris can be used for stock or soups.

Serves 4

8 medium fresh scallops, prepared weight about 350 g (12 oz)

25 g (1 oz) butter

15 ml (1 tbsp) grapeseed oil

350 g (12 oz) tail piece of red snapper, scaled and filleted

1 small shallot, skinned and chopped

350 g (12 oz) cooked whole prawns, peeled

30 ml (2 level tbsp) fresh coconut flesh, grated

15 ml (1 tbsp) fresh coconut water

30 ml (2 level tbsp) chopped parsley

30 ml (2 tbsp) thick cream

salt and freshly ground pepper

15 g (½ oz) cracker biscuits, crumbled

1. Pat the scallops dry between sheets of kitchen paper. Put the butter and oil into a shallow heat-proof casserole or browning dish and microwave on HIGH for 1½ minutes.
2. Add the scallops, piercing each with a knife point, and turn until coated in the butter-oil mixture. Cover loosely with cling film and microwave on HIGH for 1 minute, turning over halfway through cooking time. Drain and remove from the pan. Set aside.
3. Cut the snapper into 1 cm (½ inch) diagonal strips. Add these with the shallot, prawns, coconut flesh and water and microwave on HIGH, uncovered, for a further 2 minutes.
4. Stir in the parsley, halve the scallops crosswise and then replace them in the mixture and microwave on HIGH, uncovered, for 1½ minutes or until well heated.
5. Stir in the cream to the fish stew, season with salt and pepper and scatter the cracker crumbs over. Microwave on HIGH for ½–1 minute or until the sauce is hot. Serve in bowls, soup plates, scallop shells or in the centre of a mound of sweet potato or pumpkin if wished.

BERIT'S MACKEREL MOUSSES WITH CAVIAR

Moist, chunky smoked mackerel fillets (still with their own skin) should be used for this recipe as their natural creaminess is important to the texture of the dish. If you can afford to be profligate, use the 'real McCoy' – Beluga or Sevruga caviar – or choice, red jewel-like salmon caviar, in place of the inexpensive lumpfish roe. The recipe perfectly warrants it, so the decision is yours entirely. Such a simple lunch or supper recipe will please even the sternest of critics.

Serves 4

225 g (8 oz) smoked mackerel fillets, skinned

30 ml (2 level tbsp) grated horseradish

3 egg whites, at room temperature

freshly ground black pepper

60 ml (4 tbsp) double cream

60 ml (4 level tbsp) red or black lumpfish roe, salmon 'caviar' or caviar

1. Flake the mackerel and mix with the horseradish until smooth. Whisk the egg whites until soft peaks form and then fold into the fish.
2. Lightly oil 4 small 90 ml (3 fl oz) china pots, ramekins or cocottes. Spoon equal amounts of the mixture into each.

3. Microwave on HIGH, uncovered, for 3 minutes. Leave to stand for 3 minutes and then invert on to heated serving dishes.
4. Trickle a tablespoon of cream over each mousse and spoon the chosen fish roe on top. Serve hot, while they are as pretty as a picture.

See photograph page 27

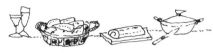

——— **SERVING TIP** ———
These little mousses make a satisfying meal with buttered bridge or wholewheat rolls, followed by a vegetable dish such as petits pois à la française.

BRANDADE WITH A COLLAR OF CUCUMBER

Somewhat similar to the Scots dish Cullen Skink yet closer to the French Brandade de Morue, these golden, hot, buttery pyramids of potato purée sting with garlic and are mellow with smoked (but not salt) cod. Each is ringed with a collar of cucumber at the base, with a pool of lemony sauce floated round the edge. Serve copious draughts of cold Chablis, Muscadet or even a Tokay d'Alsace to quench the inevitable thirst this hearty dish inspires.

Serves 4–6

700 g (1½ lb) smoked cod fillets, skin and bones removed
30 ml (2 tbsp) dry white wine
15 ml (1 tbsp) fruity olive oil
900 g (2 lb) old potatoes
75 ml (3 fl oz) creamy milk
25 g (1 oz) bunch of fresh thyme
1 fresh bay leaf, crushed
2–3 large garlic cloves, skinned and crushed
75 g (3 oz) unsalted butter
45 ml (3 tbsp) double cream
freshly ground white pepper
½ cucumber, thinly sliced

Sauce

45 ml (3 tbsp) double cream
25 g (1 oz) unsalted butter
5 ml (1 tsp) freshly squeezed lemon juice

1. Put the fish in a large, shallow heatproof dish or plate. Pour over the white wine and oil and cover loosely with cling film.
2. Microwave on HIGH for 5 minutes, turning the dish halfway through cooking time.
3. Peel the potatoes, cut into 1 cm (½ inch) cubes and put into a medium heatproof bowl with the milk, thyme and bay leaf. Cover loosely with cling film and microwave on HIGH for 10 minutes, stirring from the outside to centre halfway through cooking time. The potatoes should be tender and evenly cooked. Remove and discard the thyme and bay.
4. Using an electric hand-held mixer (or rotary beater or whisk) beat the garlic, butter and 45 ml (3 tbsp) double cream into the hot cooked potato. Add the cooked fish (and the juice) in pieces and continue to whisk until creamy and almost smooth. Season to taste.
5. Arrange pyramids or cones of the brandade on 4–6 individual serving plates and garnish with a collar of overlapping, thinly sliced cucumber around the base.
6. To make the sauce, put the cream and butter in a small bowl or jug and microwave, uncovered, on HIGH for 40 seconds. Stir in the lemon juice.
7. Microwave each serving on HIGH, uncovered, on its plate for 45 seconds to heat through, spooning a little sauce around each.

——— **COOK'S TIP** ———
If heated from cold, microwave each plate on HIGH for 2 minutes for piping hot brandade.

SEA BASS WITH PINE KERNELS

This splendid fish can be cooked simply or treated in a vigorous manner. Pine kernels, anchovies and basil accentuate the succulence of the flesh in this recipe.

Serves 4–6

1.6 kg (3½ lb) whole sea bass, prepared and gutted
100 g (4 oz) pine kernels, toasted
50 g (2 oz) can anchovy fillets, drained
30 ml (2 level tbsp) chopped fresh parsley
15 ml (1 tbsp) chopped fresh basil leaves
10 ml (2 level tsp) grated lemon rind
15 ml (1 tbsp) freshly squeezed lemon juice
30 ml (2 tbsp) fruity olive oil
freshly ground black pepper
8 cos or oak leaf lettuce leaves

1. Wash and dry the fish using kitchen paper. Pierce the eyeballs with a metal skewer. Using a sharp knife slash the fish four times crosswise at intervals on each side.
2. To toast the pine kernels spread them on a heatproof plate and microwave on HIGH, uncovered, for 4 minutes, stirring from edges towards centre halfway through cooking time.
3. Put the toasted pine kernels and anchovy fillets into a food processor or blender and process briefly to chop them roughly and blend them. Add the parsley, basil, lemon rind and juice and process again breifly to form a coarse paste.
4. Use the paste to stuff each of the 8 slashes and use any remaining to fill the gut cavity.
5. Place the fish on a large oval heatproof plate and pour over the olive oil. Season with black pepper. Cover loosely with cling film and microwave on HIGH for 12 minutes, turning the fish over halfway through cooking time.
6. Remove the cling film, tuck the lettuce leaves around the fish in a 'cradle' and tent with foil for 1–2 minutes. Remove the foil and serve whole.

SALMON AND ÉCREVISSE WITH CASTLE ROCK SAUCE

Holidays in my childhood were often spent on a farm which, in addition to sheep, ponies, cows and geese, had its own stream with freshwater crayfish.

Tiny, freshwater crayfish have always been the delight of those who love good food. In this recipe they are cooked and served with a slice of salmon and the two fish together yield a delicious stock which, heavily reduced, is the basis of a distinctive sauce. One crustacean is served complete in its vivid red shell, and the shelled tail portions become decorative garnishes for the salmon. The emptied shells are crushed and used to make the fumet with fennel stalks and shallots.

Serves 4

four 175 g (6 oz) small salmon steaks, 2.5 cm (1 inch) thick
15 ml (1 level tbsp) butter
60 ml (4 tbsp) white wine
freshly ground black pepper
8 live écrevisses or freshwater crayfish, about 450 g (1 lb)

Sauce

150 ml (¼ pint) water
150 ml (¼ pint) white wine
50 g (2 oz) Florence fennel bulb, chopped
1 shallot, skinned and chopped
10–15 whole peppercorns
30 ml (2 tbsp) sherry vinegar
15 g (½ oz) butter
15 ml (1 level tbsp) clotted Devonshire cream
salt and freshly ground black pepper
1 egg yolk

1. Arrange the salmon steaks in a lightly buttered, large, shallow heatproof dish so that the thinner ends point towards the centre of the dish.
2. Dot evenly with the 15 ml (1 level tbsp) butter, pour over the wine and sprinkle with the freshly ground black pepper. Cover with cling film and microwave on HIGH for 6 minutes, turning the dish halfway through cooking time. Then set it aside.
3. Put 4 of the écrevisses into a large, deep heatproof bowl or casserole. Pour on plenty of freshly boiling water, at least 1.7 litres (3 pints). Cover immediately with a lid and microwave on HIGH for 2 minutes. Leave to stand for 5 minutes and then strain through a colander. Repeat the same process to cook the 4 remaining écrevisses.
4. To shell 4 of the écrevisses, pull the head away from the tail and set it aside. Snap the carapace (tail shell) outwards with both hands and so remove it from the tail meat. Keep these shells and put the tail meat aside. Crush the head shells and carapace and use them to make the sauce.
5. Put all the crushed shells, the water, wine, fennel, shallot, peppercorns and sherry vinegar into a large, shallow heatproof dish. Microwave, uncovered, on HIGH for 10 minutes.
6. Pour the contents of the dish through a heatproof plastic sieve into a heatproof measuring jug. Press to squeeze out the juices and any écrevisse eggs. The yield should be about 175 ml (6 fl oz). Microwave, uncovered, on HIGH for a further 3–4 minutes or until the liquid is reduced to about 120 ml (4 fl oz).
7. Add the butter, cream, salt and freshly ground black pepper.
8. Pour a little of this mixture on to the beaten egg yolk in a separate heatproof bowl.
9. Pour the contents of this bowl back into the measuring jug. Microwave, uncovered, on HIGH for 30 seconds, stir well and, if necessary to thicken, microwave on HIGH for a further 30 seconds.
10. Arrange one salmon steak and one complete écrevisse on each serving plate. Pour a little of the sauce over each salmon portion and place one peeled écrevisse tail on top. Cover each plate with cling film and microwave on HIGH for 45 seconds, or until hot.

See photograph page 38

SMOKED SALMON AND WHITE FISH TIMBALES

When cut through, these individual timbales, or moulds, reveal two distinct layers surrounded by a 'wrapper' of smoked salmon. Each layer is topped by a perfect herb sprig kept freshly green by the rapid microwave cooking.

Serves 4

2.5 ml (½ tsp) sunflower oil

4 small fresh fennel fronds

100 g (4 oz) smoked salmon

225 g (8 oz) cod fillet, skinned and diced

2 shallots, skinned and chopped

10 ml (2 level tsp) fennel fronds

2 eggs

90 ml (6 level tbsp) strained thick Greek yogurt

1. Lightly oil 4 tiny heatproof timbales, ramekin dishes, or 4 of the hollows in a microware bun dish. Lay a fennel frond in each.
2. Using kitchen scissors, cut the smoked salmon into 4 rectangles each about 5 cm (2 inch) by 10 cm (4 inch). Place one slice across each ramekin or hollow, firming it down to touch the herb-lined base. Leave the salmon edges to hang over the rim of the dish.
3. Cut the salmon trimmings (about 25 g [1 oz]) into fine shreds using kitchen scissors.
4. Using a food processor or blender, chop the cod, shallots and the 10 ml (2 level tsp) of fennel. Add the eggs and yogurt and pulse them briefly to mix (do not over process). If using a mincer, mince the first 3 ingredients together, then beat in the eggs and yogurt until they are mixed.
5. Spoon half the mixture into the 4 prepared dishes. Take the shredded salmon trimmings and add them to the remaining mixture. Spoon this second mixture evenly over the top of each dish and tuck (or wrap) the ends of the salmon over the filling. Cover loosely with baking parchment.
6. Microwave on HIGH for 3 minutes, rotating the bun dish or rearranging the ramekins halfway through the cooking time. Leave the containers to stand for 30 seconds and then turn them out.
7. Serve hot, spooning the juices formed during cooking over the timbales.

FRUTTI DI MARE SUSPIRUS

Just as it takes a mongrel dog to sniff out a Piedmontese truffle, perhaps it takes a culinary outsider to devise such Italianate seafood morsels as these. The fish sauce, containing delectable creamy mascarpone cheese, fish juices and white wine once caused a diner at my table to sigh with pleasure, hence my name (from suspirare – 'sigh') for this dish. Of course only live scampi and mussels should be used and the squid should smell very sweet and fresh when purchased. The microwave oven helps to keep the full 'sea bouquet' of such dainties as these and preserves their appearance by minimal cooking.

Before this seafood main course why not serve Pinimonio, an antipasto of celery stalks dipped into good olive oil, then salt and freshly ground pepper.

Serves 4

8 live scampi or Dublin Bay prawns

900 g (2 lb) live mussels

75 ml (3 fl oz) Soave or white Merlot wine

1 shallot, skinned and chopped

4 large squid, about 15 cm (6 inch) body length

225 g (8 oz) [8–12] cooked, cracked crab claws, on their shell

2 spring onions, trimmed

30 ml (2 level tbsp) ricotta cheese

3 star anise seed heads

15 ml (1 tbsp) fennel fronds

30 ml (2 tbsp) reserved mussel liquor

salt and pepper to taste

Sauce

150 ml ($\frac{1}{4}$ pint) mussel and squid cooking liquor

60 ml (4 level tbsp) mascarpone cheese

15 ml (1 tbsp) lemon juice

30 ml (2 level tbsp) chopped fresh parsley

Garnish

1 lemon in wedges or slices

1. Put the scampi or prawns into a large, deep heatproof bowl or casserole. Quickly pour on freshly boiling water. Cover with a lid and microwave on HIGH for 2 minutes. Leave to stand for 5–8 minutes, then drain through a colander, cover with cling film and refrigerate.
2. Put the scrubbed mussels in a large, shallow heatproof dish. Pour on the wine and add the shallot. Cover with cling film and microwave on HIGH for 2 minutes. Remove and reserve those mussels which have opened. Cover the dish and microwave on HIGH for a further 2 minutes. Again remove and reserve the cooked open mussels. If any mussels remain closed, microwave for a further minute and then discard the unopened mussels. Pour off the mussel and wine liquor through a fine plastic (or muslin lined) sieve and reserve.
3. Pull off and discard the empty half shells, reserving the mussels, each upon its shell. Cover with cling film and refrigerate.
4. Wash the squid and tug apart the head and tentacle section from the body sac. Rinse under running water to empty out all contents, including grit, discarding the transparent back-bone. Cut off the tentacle section from each squid and use it partially to stuff each body sac. Remove the cooked flesh from all but four crab claws. Discard the emptied claws. Chop the spring onions finely and mix with the crab and ricotta. Break apart the star anise heads to release their aromatic seeds, then crush these and add to the crab and ricotta mixture with the fennel fronds. Season to taste and fill the squid body sacs loosely with this mixture. Push the fleshy end of one reserved crab claw into the opening of each stuffed squid.
5. Position the 4 stuffed squid on a shallow heatproof dish with the claws pointing towards the centre. To prevent them from splitting or bursting during cooking, pierce each squid 3 or 4 times with the point of a sharp knife. Pour on some of the reserved mussel cooking liquor, cover with cling film and microwave on HIGH for 3 minutes, giving the dish a quarter turn halfway

through cooking time. Leave to stand for 10 minutes, uncovered, then cover with cling film and refrigerate. Add any cooking liquids to the reserved mussel cooking liquor.

6. Measure the mussel liquor and add more wine if necessary to make 150 ml (¼ pint). Blend the liquor, mascarpone cheese, lemon juice and parsley smoothly together and microwave, uncovered, on HIGH for 1 minute or until hot. Allow to stand for 1 minute, taste and adjust seasonings.

7. On each serving plate put one stuffed squid, 6–8 (or a quarter share) of the mussels, 2 whole cooked scampi and a small heatproof china or glass pot containing the sauce. Cover each plate with cling film and microwave them one at a time on HIGH for 1 minute or until hot. Serve with lemon and crusty brown bread.

SEAFARERS' SOUP WITH PERNOD

This sustaining soup of herbs, saffron and tomato flavours, with a selection of available seafish, is a meal in itself. Serve it by the steaming bowlful with some Fougasse or other crusty French bread to mop up the brilliantly colourful liquid. A final addition of Pernod imparts a faintly aniseed scent to the whole and is a pleasing refinement.

Serves 4

300 ml (½ pint) water
300 ml (½ pint) white wine such as Entre deux Mers or Meursault
100 g (4 oz) onion, skinned and quartered
900 g (2 lb) prepared fresh fish on the bone (such as turbot, halibut, hake, red mullet or mackerel)
25 g (1 oz) bunch parsley stalks
15 g (½ oz) bunch fresh thyme sprigs
1.25 ml (¼ tsp) powdered saffron
10 ml (2 level tsp) tomato purée
1.25 ml (¼ tsp) tabasco or hot chilli sauce
225 g (8 oz) bulb of fennel, sliced lengthwise
225 g (8 oz) leek, thickly sliced
50 g (2 oz) mange tout peas, prepared
30 ml (2 tbsp) Pernod (or similar liquor)
freshly ground black pepper
salt to taste

1. Put the water and wine into a large heatproof bowl with the onion.
2. Remove the bones from the fish and add them to the bowl with the fish trimmings, parsley stalks and thyme. Cover with cling film and microwave on HIGH for 7 minutes.
3. Strain the stock through a colander back into the large heatproof bowl, stirring in the saffron, tomato purée and tabasco.
4. Add the sliced fennel and leek, cover with cling film and microwave on HIGH for 3½ minutes, stirring once halfway through the cooking time.
5. Cut the fish into 5 cm (2 inch) chunks and add to the bowl. Cover and microwave on HIGH for 4 minutes, stirring carefully halfway through cooking time so that the fish pieces still retain their shape.
6. Stir in the mange tout, Pernod, and black pepper and salt to taste. Leave to stand, covered, for 1 minute before ladling into the serving bowls or soup plates.

——— **SERVING TIP** ———
Fougasse is slashed and shaped regional bread available from some boulangeries and specialist bread shops. If it is unavailable use any crusty, thin French bread.

P·O·U·L·T·R·Y
A·N·D G·A·M·E

EMBROIDERED CHICKEN TARRAGONA

Prettily moistened, seasoned and enhanced by individual strips of cured ham, these boneless skinned chicken breasts cook in a rich and velvety sauce. The embroidered effect is achieved by using a rounded knife blade to insert each folded strip of ham into the prepared incisions. Threaded from opposite directions, the ends look like loose ribbons.

Serves 4

2 slices Parma ham

4 suprêmes of chicken, 100–150 g (4–5 oz) each

15 ml (1 tbsp) grapeseed oil

15 ml (1 level tbsp) butter

15 ml (1 tbsp) white wine

4 sprigs of fresh tarragon or tarragon in vinegar (drained)

15 ml (1 tbsp) very thick cream

freshly ground black pepper

1. Preheat a 20 cm (8 inch) browning dish for 5–6 minutes or according to the manufacturer's instructions.
2. Cut each piece of ham crosswise into 8 strips, using scissors.
3. With a small, sharp knife blade, push crosswise through the top layer of each suprême until the knife tip shows (as if making a stitch with a needle). Repeat in 3 more places to make a total of 4 incisions down each breast.
4. Using a small, blunt-ended knife, push or 'weave' the strips of ham through each incision or 'stitch'. This should leave 2 ham ends hanging over the meat to moisten it while it cooks.
5. Add the oil and butter to the browning dish.

Quickly brown each side of the chicken breasts.
6. Add the wine, tarragon, cream and pepper, stirring to dislodge any fragments from the dish. Microwave, uncovered, on HIGH for 7 minutes giving the dish a half turn halfway through cooking time.
7. Serve the chicken in a pool of its sauce.

See photograph page 45

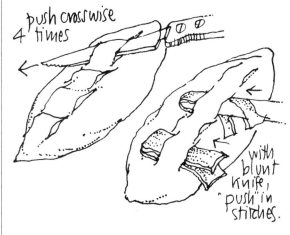

push crosswise 4 times

with blunt knife, "push" in stitches.

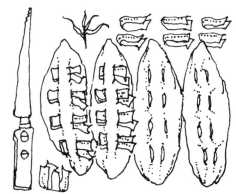

───── **SERVING TIP** ─────
Try serving the chicken with spicy glazed baby onions (page 70) and follow with a seasonal green salad.

STEAMED CHICKEN MOUSSES PANACHÉES

These boneless, skinned breasts of corn-fed chicken, cooked as two variously coloured layers in four china pots, are turned out and served with a tasty though simple sauce. Fresh tarragon, if not available, could be replaced by tarragon preserved in vinegar, drained. The mango chutney used is taken from the recipe on page 91.

Serves 4

4 fresh tarragon sprigs
four 100 g (4 oz) corn fed chicken suprêmes, roughly chopped
freshly ground black pepper
45 ml (3 tbsp) vermouth bianco
2 egg whites, at room temperature
120 ml (8 level tbsp) double cream
30 ml (2 level tbsp) chopped fresh tarragon
15 ml (1 level tbsp) mango chutney (page 91)
5 ml (1 level tsp) paprika

Sauce

30 ml (2 level tbsp) lemon mayonnaise
salt to taste

1. Butter 4 individual 150 ml ($\frac{1}{4}$ pint) heatproof oval or round pots, terrines or ramekins and lay a fresh tarragon sprig in the base of each.
2. Put the chicken into a food processor or blender and work briefly until smooth. Add the pepper and vermouth and process again in short bursts.
3. Whisk the egg whites until soft peaks form and add to the chicken mixture. Process again briefly until evenly blended. Whip 90 ml (6 level tbsp) of the cream and fold it into the mixture.
4. Divide the mixture into two halves, keeping one half aside. Gently smooth the other half into the individual pots. Cover with a layer of freshly chopped tarragon.
5. Add to the reserved chicken mixture the mango chutney and 2.5 ml ($\frac{1}{2}$ level tsp) of the paprika. Cover the first layer of chicken and tarragon with this second mixture, pressing it firmly into place.
6. Place the 4 dishes inside a roasting bag and arrange them in the microwave oven so that each is equidistant from the centre. Loosely secure the roasting bag with a rubber band or non-metallic tie. Microwave on HIGH for 6 minutes, rearranging the position of the oven bag and the dishes after 3 minutes. Remove from the oven and leave to stand, still enclosed, for 5 minutes.
7. Meanwhile, make the sauce. Combine the mayonnaise with the remaining 30 ml (2 tbsp) of cream and 2.5 ml ($\frac{1}{2}$ level tsp) of paprika in a small heatproof serving dish or sauceboat. Add salt to taste and microwave on HIGH for 30 seconds, or until heated.
8. To serve, slice each terrine crosswise into 5 or 6 pieces and spoon some sauce on to each plate.

——— **SERVING TIP** ———
This delicate dish is excellent followed by a crisp, mixed seasonal red-leaf salad with apple and nut garnish.

CHICKEN THIGHS MACADAMIA

Plump, boned and skinned chicken meat here encloses a stuffing of incomparably delicious fresh dates and Gruyère cheese. When sliced through to serve, the chicken shows the still-green flesh of the dates, with the cheese inside. The accompanying sauce, a delicate mauve-pink, contains nut oil, whole macadamia nuts and red wine, and is carefully enriched by a liaison of egg yolk and cream. A sophisticated treat and a lovely party piece, this dish merits the drinking of a good claret.

Serves 4

8 whole fresh dates

25 g (1 oz) Gruyère cheese, cut into 8 strips

8 chicken thighs, boned and skinned, 550 g (1¼ lb)

30 ml (2 tbsp) hazelnut oil

2 garlic cloves, skinned and crushed

150 ml (¼ pint) red Bordeaux wine

1 egg yolk, at room temperature

30 ml (2 tbsp) rich double cream

50 g (2 oz) roast, salted macadamia nuts

2.5 ml (½ level tsp) salt

Garnish (optional)

fresh herb sprigs

1. Split the dates lengthwise to remove the stones. Fill each cavity with a strip of Gruyère and enclose the cheese inside.
2. Preheat a 25 cm (10 inch) browning dish on HIGH for 8 minutes. Lay the chicken thighs out flat, skinned side downwards. Place a stuffed date on the centre of each piece of chicken, then wrap the chicken round it to enclose the stuffing completely, securing each thigh with a wooden cocktail stick.
3. Pour the hazelnut oil into the preheated browning dish and quickly add the chicken thighs with the smooth, rounded sides downwards. Microwave, uncovered, on HIGH for 2 minutes. Carefully turn over each chicken thigh and rearrange in the dish.
4. Add the crushed garlic and red wine and cover with cling film. Microwave on HIGH for 6 minutes, giving the dish a quarter turn halfway through the cooking time.
5. Carefully remove the cooked chicken from the liquid and set aside to cool slightly. In a separate bowl, stir the egg yolk and cream together. Add 15 ml (1 tbsp) of the hot wine stock to this and then pour the contents of the bowl back into the browning dish. Add the macadamia nuts and microwave on HIGH, uncovered, for 1–1½ minutes to thicken the sauce, stirring from the edges to the centre halfway through cooking time. The sauce should be velvety textured. Add salt to taste.
6. Allow 2 stuffed chicken thighs for each serving, sliced and arranged on the plates in a pool of the sauce. Cover with cling film and heat the individual servings for 30 seconds on HIGH, before taking to the table.
7. Garnish with fresh chervil, or other herb sprigs if wished.

COOK'S TIP

Macadamia nuts have a unique taste and are truly worth seeking out at good delicatessens, supermarkets or specialist food stores. If wished, the dish can be made early in the day, chilled, and heated again just before serving.

Glazed Baby Onions (page 70) with succulent Embroidered Chicken Tarragona (page 42).

Left: Magrets de Canard with Peppered Apple Sauce (page 51).
Top left: Arcadian Venison (page 53).
Top right: Bacon and Kidney Kebab with Sauce Christina (page 56).
Above left: Sliced Loin of Lamb with Salsify and Mushrooms (page 61).
Above right: Roast Beef Anchoïade (page 57).

Veal Medallions with Juniper (page 65) and cloud ear mushrooms.

SPATCHCOCKED POUSSINS WITH KUMQUATS

Fresh kumquats (often available in ethnic food markets, good supermarkets and speciality food stores) give real charm to this recipe. But satsumas, clementines or mandarin oranges can be used as second best. The freshly squeezed orange juice and fresh marjoram or oregano leaves are, however, irreplaceable.

Serves 4

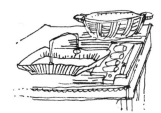

two 450 g (1 lb) prepared poussins

30 ml (2 level tbsp) butter, at room temperature

60 ml (4 tbsp) grapeseed oil

100 g (4 oz) fresh kumquats, thinly sliced crosswise

15 ml (1 level tbsp) fresh marjoram or oregano leaves

120 ml (8 tbsp) fresh orange juice

salt and freshly ground black pepper to taste

Garnish (optional)

fresh marjoram or oregano sprigs

1. Using kitchen scissors or poultry shears, cut each poussin down the backbone and open out flat like a book. Placing one bird skin side upwards, cover with cling film and beat 5 or 6 times using a cutlet bat or rolling pin to flatten well. Repeat this process with the second bird.
2. Insert 2 wooden skewers crosswise through each bird, threading one through the wings and breast and the second through the drumsticks and lower breast.
3. Preheat a 25 cm (10 inch) browning dish for 7–8 minutes, or according to the manufacturer's instructions.
4. Add half the butter, half the oil and one bird to the preheated browning dish and microwave, uncovered, for 1 minute on HIGH. Using tongs, carefully turn the bird over and microwave for a further 1 minute.

5. Wipe the pan using absorbent kitchen paper. Add the remaining measure of oil. Repeat the entire process for the second poussin (but preheat the dish for only 3–4 minutes, or according to the manufacturer's instructions).
6. Add the kumquats, marjoram and orange juice to the dish and arrange the 2 birds on it so that they overlap. Cover with a lid and microwave on HIGH for 10 minutes, basting and rearranging the position of the birds after 5 minutes. Leave to stand, covered, for 2–3 minutes.
7. To serve, remove the skewers and cut each bird in half lengthwise down the centre of the breast. Spoon on some of the sauce and garnish with a marjoram or oregano sprig if wished.

—— **SERVING TIP** ——

This recipe is sufficient for four modest appetites but will satisfy only two hungry gourmets.

CORN-FED CHICKEN PAUPIETTES WITH MUSTARD BUTTER

Parcels of chicken twice wrapped, once with cured raw beef, and once with fresh green spinach, make a diverting dish. The hot mustardy 'stuffing' may shock the taste buds but is well worth trying. Coppa crudo (cured pork) provides an alternative, not exactly a substitute, if no Bresaola (cured beef fillet) is available.

Serves 4

2 large, 225 g (8 oz) breasts of corn-feed chicken, boned and skinned

25 g (1 oz) butter

30 ml (2 level tbsp) prepared hot English mustard

1 garlic clove, skinned and crushed

15 ml (1 level tbsp) chopped fresh flat leaf parsley

salt and freshly ground black pepper

8 wafer thin slices of Bresaola or coppa crudo

8 medium spinach or spinach beet leaves

5 ml (1 tsp) olive oil

1. Cut each chicken breast across into quarters. Slice each quarter through crosswise into halves and spread both sides with a well blended mixture of the butter, mustard, garlic, parsley and seasonings. Sandwich the chicken pieces back together and enfold each chicken paupiette in a slice of the Bresaola or coppa crudo.
2. Making a narrow V-shape, cut away the central stalks from the bases of the spinach leaves. Place each meat-wrapped paupiette in the centre of a leaf and fold over all the edges to enclose the chicken completely.
3. Arrange the paupiettes in a circle round the edge of a heatproof plate. Brush lightly with the oil, then cover with cling film and microwave for 6 minutes on HIGH. Leave to stand for 1 minute, uncover and serve immediately.

----- SERVING TIP -----
Serve two paupiettes on each plate, with purée of celeriac, potato, carrot or pumpkin and a crisp green vegetable.

TURKEY FUNDADOR WITH CHESTNUTS AND AVOCADO

Chestnuts, perfectly cooked by microwave oven inside their own, twice-pierced skins, and without added water, taste particularly delicious. They are sweet, moist and their skins peel easily.

I try to keep some Fundador or Metaxa brandy in my kitchen after holidays abroad. These light, fruity brandies can do wonders for many savoury and sweet dishes. The emphasis on nuts with turkey seems to me very Spanish, so try serving this dish with some simply cooked rice.

Serves 4

350 g (12 oz) fresh chestnuts

350 g (12 oz) turkey fillets

45 ml (3 level tbsp) clear honey

60 ml (4 tbsp) Fundador or other brandy

1 medium, ripe avocado, about 175 g (6 oz)

150 ml ($\frac{1}{4}$ pint) water

15 ml (1 tbsp) garlic or other vinegar

10 ml (2 level tsp) cornflour

30 ml (2 tbsp) grapeseed or olive oil

1 medium onion

1 small red pepper

1 red chilli

50 g (2 oz) roast cashew nuts

15 ml (1 level tbsp) chopped fresh parsley

salt and freshly ground black pepper

1. To shell the chestnuts, pierce each in two places with a skewer. Put them on a plate and microwave, 175 g (6 oz) at a time, uncovered, on HIGH for $1\frac{1}{2}$ minutes. Remove and discard the shells. Repeat with the remaining chestnuts.
2. Slice the turkey fillets diagonally into thin strips. Place in a bowl and add the honey and Fundador. Leave to marinate for 15 minutes.
3. Meanwhile, halve the avocado and remove the stone. Scoop out the flesh from one half and quickly mash or purée with the water, garlic vinegar and cornflour, using a food processor, blender or fork.
4. Preheat a 25 cm (10 inch) browning dish on HIGH for 8 minutes, or according to the manufacturer's instructions.

5. Add the oil to the browning dish and then the turkey strips, reserving the marinade. Stir well and add the onion, red pepper and red chilli. Microwave, uncovered, on HIGH for 2 minutes, stirring halfway through cooking time.

6. Add the reserved marinade and microwave, uncovered, for a further 2 minutes on HIGH.

7. Add the cashews, peeled chestnuts, avocado pulp and the diced flesh of the remaining avocado half. Stir well and microwave, uncovered, on HIGH for 2–3 minutes, or until the sauce is hot and thickened.

8. Scatter with the chopped parsley and season well with salt and freshly ground black pepper.

MAGRETS DE CANARD WITH PEPPERED APPLE SAUCE

The name of this recipe refers to those heavily fleshed ducks from certain areas of France. These 'smothered' ducks should be used for the following recipe, rather than their English equivalents. Only the breast meat is used and when cooked it is firm, generous and pinkish red, almost like steak in texture. These days many good supermarkets, game suppliers and even delicatessens sell Magrets de Canard, usually in pairs. The strongly flavoured sauce in this recipe counteracts the richness of the duck, and the dark honey glaze gives a very professional-looking effect, to say nothing of its taste.

Serves 4

two 250 g (9 oz) breasts of French-reared duck
30 ml (2 tbsp) liquid honey
freshly ground black pepper
15 ml (1 tbsp) virgin olive oil
15 ml (1 tbsp) walnut oil
two 100 g (4 oz) Worcester Pearmain apples, cored and sliced
finely grated rind and squeezed juice of 1 fresh lime
120 ml (4 fl oz) white wine
5 ml (1 level tsp) green peppercorns
5 ml (1 level tsp) cornflour

1. Preheat a 25 cm (10 inch) browning dish for 8 minutes, or according to the manufacturer's instructions.

2. Thoroughly dry the duck breasts in absorbent kitchen paper. Brush or spread the honey over them and quickly sprinkle with black pepper.

3. Quickly pour the olive and walnut oils into the hot browning dish and carefully place the breasts, skin side downwards, in the dish. Microwave, uncovered, on HIGH for 1½ minutes. Turn the duck breasts over carefully, and add the apples, lime juice and rind, wine and green peppercorns. Microwave on HIGH for 4 minutes.

4. Remove the breasts from the sauce, slice them lengthwise and keep warm. Using a slotted spoon, separate the apples and peppercorns from the liquid and arrange on a serving platter with the roast duck. Add the cornflour, blended with 15 ml (1 tbsp) cold water, to the liquid in the dish. Stir well and microwave, uncovered, on HIGH for 1½ minutes until the sauce is thickened and hot.

5. To serve, pour a little of the sauce around the duck and serve the remainder separately.

See photograph page 46

───────── SERVING TIP ─────────
A really frivolous salad of mesclun mixture would be a delicious accompaniment, as would oak-leaf lettuce or dandelion (or a mixture of all three) in a cream and lemon juice dressing.

GLAZED PARTRIDGE ON A PASTA NEST

Plump-fleshed partridge halves are served here on a tangled 'nest' of wholewheat pasta. The sauce, fruit based and syrupy, becomes an attractive glaze. Take care when roasting meat, poultry or game in an oven bag that the juices are removed part way through cooking time. Otherwise the food cooks too slowly and by moist heat, which also affects browning.

Serves 4

225 g (8 oz) fresh wholewheat tagliatelle, prepared as for Herb Garnished Fresh Tagliatelle (page 17)

two 425 g (15 oz) prepared young partridges

25 g (1 oz) butter

2 garlic cloves, skinned and chopped

10 ml (2 level tsp) chopped fresh parsley

freshly ground black pepper

4 rashers back bacon (smoked)

Glaze

60 ml (4 tbsp) guava conserve or jelly

20 ml (4 tsp) cherry vinegar (or other fruit vinegar)

2.5 ml ($\frac{1}{2}$ level tsp) Worcestershire sauce

1. Dry the insides of the partridges with absorbent kitchen paper.
2. Mix together the butter, garlic and parsley and insert half the mixture into the body cavity of each partridge. Grind black pepper over the birds, then wrap 2 rashers of bacon around each bird, trussing securely with string.
3. Put the birds (breasts upwards and facing in opposite directions) inside an oven bag and stand on a roasting rack. Loosely tie the bag with non-metal ties, string or a rubber band.
4. Microwave on MEDIUM (60%) for 9 minutes and then pour all the accumulated juices from the bag into the roasting rack. Give the rack a half turn and microwave on MEDIUM (60%) for a further 9 minutes.
5. Tent the birds in foil and leave them to stand for 5–8 minutes.
6. Pour the accumulated juices from the roasting rack into a medium, heatproof bowl. Add the guava conserve, cherry vinegar and Worcestershire sauce. Pour in any extra juices

cut bird length-wise in two then.....

arrange "nest" of pasta for each.

which have seeped from the body cavity during standing time. Microwave, uncovered, on HIGH for 3 minutes, stirring frequently so that the conserve dissolves evenly.
7. Since pasta cools down quickly it will be necessary to reheat the tagliatelle. Do this by covering the dish with cling film and microwave on HIGH for about 1 minute, or until hot.
8. Halve each bird lengthwise and discard the string. Serve each half-partridge 'nestling' on a circle of the finished pasta and pour some of the fruit glaze over each serving.

GLENMORANGIE GROUSE WITH GRAVY

This recipe selects those mature birds whose fine flavour makes them suitable for casseroles, yet requires them to be cooked for a very short time indeed. The herb-scented juices are treated simply (slightly thickened with a beurre manié) and the evanescent afterglow from a good malt whisky provides a finishing touch. If you are not already an afficionado of grouse or are, perhaps, sampling its flavour for the first time, then be warned, this recipe may not be for you! Microwave ovens seem to develop, rather than subdue, the distinctive flavour of this singular bird.

Serves 2

two 275 g (10 oz) prepared casserole grouse

15 ml (1 tbsp) walnut oil

15 g (½ oz) butter

2 fresh bay leaves, crushed

4 juniper berries, crushed

100 ml (4 fl oz) chicken stock (see page 20)

1 shallot, skinned and chopped

Beurre manié

10 ml (2 level tsp) butter

10 ml (2 level tsp) flour

15 g (½ oz) butter

15 ml (1 tbsp) malt whisky

5 ml (1 tsp) lemon juice

salt to taste

1. Preheat a 25 cm (10 inch) browning dish for 8 minutes. Halve each grouse lengthwise using kitchen scissors.
2. Add the walnut oil and butter to the preheated browning dish and quickly add the 4 pieces of grouse, skin side downwards. Add the bay leaves and crushed juniper berries and microwave, uncovered, on HIGH for 1½ minutes.
3. Use tongs to turn over the grouse pieces, then add the chicken stock and chopped shallot. Cover with a lid or cling film and microwave on HIGH for 6 minutes. Remove the halved grouse from the dish and set aside in tented foil.
4. Blend the butter and flour to a paste and add, in small pieces, to the sauce. Stir well and microwave on HIGH for 2 minutes or until it is thickened and very hot. Stir in the whisky, the 15 g (½ oz) measure of butter and the lemon juice.
5. Season with salt to taste and serve each portion of grouse with the sauce to accompany it.

ARCADIAN VENISON

Traditional this recipe is not; neither is it a huge, hearty dish; but it is most certainly enticing. The still pink meat has an amethyst sauce, coloured by golden flowery Moscatel wine and the skins of the dappled Napoleon type Chasselas grapes.

Leg of venison is frequently boned, cut and rolled into smaller joints, many of which are wrapped in pork (barding) fat to prevent dryness during cooking and to add flavour, as in this recipe. For perfect results, order or select a slender joint if possible, rather than a wide, compact shape. Oyster and plum sauces can both be found in specialist, Asian supermarkets and sometimes in ethnic foodmarkets.

Serves 4

30 ml (2 tbsp) grapeseed oil

700 g (1½ lb) joint of leg of venison, rolled and barded with pork fat

75 g (3 oz) onion, skinned and chopped

1 garlic clove, skinned and crushed

120 ml (4 fl oz) Moscatel wine

225 g (8 oz) Chasselas grapes, halved and seeded

15 ml (1 tbsp) oyster sauce

5 ml (1 tsp) plum sauce

5 ml (1 level tsp) fécule or potato starch

30 ml (2 tbsp) stock

salt and freshly ground black pepper to season

1. Preheat a 25 cm (10 inch) browning dish for 7 minutes, or according to the manufacturer's instructions. Pour in the oil and quickly add the venison joint. Microwave for 45 seconds on HIGH, uncovered. Using tongs, carefully turn the joint over and microwave, uncovered, for a further 45 seconds to brown it.
2. Add the onion, garlic, moscatel, prepared grapes and the oyster and plum sauces to the dish. Cover with a lid and microwave on MEDIUM (60%) for 15 minutes, giving the dish a quarter turn 3 times during cooking time. Remove the joint, tent with foil and leave it to stand for 15 minutes.
3. Blend the potato starch with the stock and add to the liquid and fruit. Stir gently. Microwave, uncovered, on HIGH for 2 minutes, stirring from the edges to the centre once or twice. Season to taste and serve the sauce with the sliced venison and perhaps an aromatic herb such as rue.

See photograph page 47

———— SERVING TIP ————
Traditional embellishments for venison include fruit jellies, watercress and crisp straw potatoes or game chips.

M·E·A·T

SWEETBREADS WITH CHANTERELLES AND KIWI FRUIT

The pastel tones of this lunch or supper dish are as unusual as the blend of flavours. Fresh sweetbreads must be used in this recipe but if fresh chanterelles are not in season, good quality chanterelles (or girolles) purchased in glass jars can be drained and substituted satisfactorily. Use a good homemade stock in order to give distinction to the sauce (page 20). Kiwi fruit has a refreshing astringency and also contains substances which tenderise meat. The segments of uncooked fruit are delicious as a garnish.

Serves 4

450 g (1 lb) lambs' sweetbreads, halved

120 ml (4 fl oz) light stock (page 20)

120 ml (4 fl oz) Riesling

6–8 parsley stalks

6 black peppercorns

60 ml (4 tbsp) double cream

75 g (3 oz) fresh chanterelle mushrooms, halved

two 75 g (3 oz) kiwi fruit, skinned

15 ml (1 level tbsp) chopped fresh chives

1. Rinse the halved sweetbreads and put in a heatproof ring mould, dish or casserole. To prevent them from splitting during cooking, pierce each sweetbread portion in several places.
2. Add the stock, wine, parsley stalks and peppercorns and cover with cling film or a lid. Microwave on HIGH for 9–10 minutes or until firm and tender.
3. Strain the contents of the dish through a colander or sieve, keeping aside the sweetbreads and discarding the parsley stalks. Reserve the cooking liquor and return it to the dish and microwave, uncovered, on HIGH for 5 minutes or until it is well reduced and syrupy.
4. Add the cream and chanterelles and stir gently. Microwave on HIGH, uncovered, for 2 minutes, giving the dish a quarter turn halfway through cooking time.
5. Put the sweetbreads back into the dish and add one kiwi fruit, sliced thinly, and the chives. Microwave again, uncovered, for a final minute or until heated thoroughly.
6. Serve with the remaining kiwi fruit, sliced into segments, as a garnish. Accompany with light crusty French bread, herbed rice or stir-fried noodles.

girolles

MOUSSELINE VOUVRAY DE CERVELLE AUX CÈPES

It is essential, I feel, to purchase delicate textured offal (such as lambs' brains) in a perfect state and absolutely fresh, not frozen. The sauce in which these tiny brain 'puffs' are served contains that luxury — fresh cèpes. It is voluptuously rich and a remarkable partner for such little delicacies. If you have never been tempted to try brains before, this recipe may attract you to a delectable, but most neglected, dish.

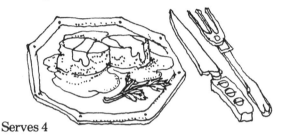

Serves 4

4 sets lambs' brains, 375–400 g (13–14 oz) in all

15 ml (1 tbsp) lemon juice

150 ml (¼ pint) Vouvray or similar white wine

1 shallot, skinned and sliced

10–12 parsley stalks, tied with string

25 g (1 oz) butter

50 g (2 oz) fresh cèpes (boletus) fungi, thinly sliced

30 ml (2 tbsp) thick Jersey cream

2 eggs, at room temperature

salt and freshly ground black pepper

15 ml (1 level tbsp) chopped fresh parsley

Garnish

4 sprigs flat leaf parsley

1. Barely cover the brains with cold water, add the lemon juice and leave for 15 minutes. Drain away the water and halve each set of brains lengthwise, discarding any dark tissues or bone fragments.
2. Put the meat into a shallow heatproof dish or casserole. Add the wine, shallot and parsley stalks. Cover with cling film and microwave on HIGH for 7 minutes. Allow to stand for several minutes.
3. Remove one brain portion and halve it through crosswise: it should be a beige-white colour with no pronounced pinkness inside. If it still appears pink, cook until the meat has changed colour. Halve the remaining brain portions crosswise and dry them on kitchen paper.
4. Remove and discard the parsley stalks from the cooking liquid. Microwave the liquid, uncovered, on HIGH for 5 minutes or until it reduces to about half. Pour into a separate jug and reserve.
5. To the same heatproof dish add the butter and microwave, uncovered, on HIGH for 1 minute or until the butter melts. Stir in the cèpes (both cap and stalk) and toss to coat. Microwave, uncovered, on HIGH for 1 minute, add the reduced liquid and the cream and shake or stir gently to blend the sauce ingredients.
6. Separate the egg yolks from the whites. Whisk the whites and salt, using an electric or rotary beater, until stiff peaks form. Whisk the yolks with 15 ml (1 tbsp) warm water and black pepper for 2–3 minutes or until the yolks are pale and frothy and have tripled in volume. Add the chopped parsley and carefully fold the egg whites evenly into the yolks to make the soufflé-omelette mixture.
7. Grease and base line an 8 hole microware bun pan or 8 small, 75 ml (3 fl oz) heatproof pots or cocottes. Put 1 spoonful of the egg mixture into the base of each. Put 2 of the 16 pieces of halved brains, cross-cut face downwards, into each container. Divide the remaining egg mixture and smooth equal amounts over each pot.
8. Microwave on HIGH for 4 minutes, giving the pan (or dishes) a quarter turn halfway through cooking time. Allow to stand and immediately microwave the sauce, uncovered, on HIGH for 2 minutes. After standing, the brain soufflés should shrink slightly from the edges. Loosen and invert them on to a large flat plate, removing the lining papers if necessary.
9. Spoon a little hot sauce over and around each pair of soufflés. Garnish with flat leaf parsley sprigs.

BACON AND KIDNEY KEBABS WITH SAUCE CHRISTINA

Offal cooked in the microwave oven retains a full-bodied flavour and provides a delightful contrast when served in a delicate avocado sauce. One kebab and its sauce makes a perfect starter. for a main course dish, twice the kebab quantities would be needed. A glass of Mercurey adds the final touch when serving.

Serves 4

Sauce

1 medium avocado, stoned and peeled
15 ml (1 tbsp) clear honey
1 ripe guava, peeled
45 ml (3 tbsp) white dessert wine
2.5 ml ($\frac{1}{2}$ level tsp) salt

Kebabs

4 rashers streaky bacon (smoked), rinded
4 lambs' kidneys, skinned, cored and quartered

Garnish (optional)

fresh avocado slices
fresh chervil or flat leaf parsley

1. To make the sauce, chop the prepared avocado flesh and place in a food processor or blender with the honey. Roughly chop the guava and place in a small heatproof bowl with the wine. Cover with cling film and microwave on HIGH for 2 minutes.
2. Add the guava fruit, while hot, to the avocado and process until smooth. Add salt to taste and sieve to remove the seeds.

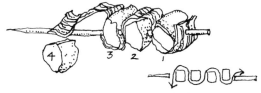

3. To make the kebabs, thread the bacon and kidney quarters on to 4 short wooden or bamboo skewers. See that the bacon remains in one piece as it is threaded down the length of the skewer, over and under the kidney quarters and partly enclosing them.

4. Place the kebabs on a rack suspended over a dish to catch the dripping juices. Microwave on HIGH for 6 minutes, turning halfway through the cooking time. Leave to stand for 1 minute (the colour deepens in this period) then dip the kebabs in their dripped juices before serving.
5. Serve each kebab in a pool of the avocado sauce, garnished with slices of fresh avocado and a herb sprig if wished.

See photograph page 47

LAMBS' TONGUES QUINLIVAN IN RAISIN SAUCE

Not all butchers salt or brine meats these days. I am fortunate to have one such old-fashioned and obliging butcher nearby in Portobello Road. Ask your own butcher whether these lambs' tongues need much soaking to prevent them producing an over-salty sauce.

Serves 4

8 brined lambs' tongues
1 large onion, skinned and sliced
3 fresh bay leaves
15 ml (1 level tbsp) fresh sage leaves
30 ml (2 level tbsp) parsley stalks, chopped

Sauce

200 ml ($\frac{1}{3}$ pint) fresh orange juice
100 g (4 oz) seedless raisins
10 ml (2 level tsp) arrowroot

Garnish

shredded rind of 1 orange
flesh of 1 orange, sliced

1. Arrange a layer of lambs' tongues in a medium, heatproof casserole dish. Add the sliced onion, bay leaves, sage leaves, parsley stalks and 450 ml (15 fl oz) boiling water. Cover with a lid or cling film and microwave on MEDIUM (60%) for 50 minutes, or until the tongues are tender and

can be skinned easily.

2. Remove the tongues and set aside. Strain the stock (there should be about 300 ml [½ pint]) into a medium, heatproof bowl and microwave, uncovered, on HIGH for 5 minutes to reduce.

3. Meanwhile, skin the tongues and remove any tough tissues at the base. Slice each tongue in half lengthwise and set aside. Add the orange juice and raisins to the stock and microwave, uncovered, on HIGH for 5 minutes.

4. To thicken the sauce, mix the arrowroot with 30 ml (2 tbsp) cold water. Stir into the sauce and microwave, uncovered, on HIGH for 30–45 seconds.

5. Place the sliced tongues in a heatproof serving dish, pour on the hot sauce and microwave, uncovered, on HIGH for 1 minute to heat through.

6. Serve sprinkled with shreds of orange rind and garnished with orange slices.

ROAST BEEF ANCHOÏADE

Basic timings and necessary techniques for cooking boneless beef in the microwave oven are shown below. Make sure that the meat is at room temperature and well dried before it starts to cook. To monitor the internal temperature of meats, special microwave thermometers can be used, and certain microwave ovens contain probes. The timings shown below are, however, an excellent guide.

Serves 4–6

1.5 g (3¼ lb) boneless rolled beef (such as topside)

50 g (2 oz) can anchovy fillets

freshly ground black pepper

15 ml (1 tbsp) fruity olive oil

15 ml (1 tbsp) blackcurrant vinegar

75 ml (5 tbsp) red wine vinegar

5 ml (1 level tsp) cornflour

30 ml (2 tbsp) stock

Garnish (optional)

chopped fresh parsley

1. Preheat a 25 cm (10 inch) browning dish for 8 minutes, or according to the manufacturer's instructions. Using a small pointed knife, pierce the meat (in a series of 3 parallel lines down its length) to a depth of 5 cm (2 inches).

2. Drain the anchovy fillets and halve them crosswise. Using the handle of a teaspoon, push the halved anchovy fillets deep into the incisions. Dry the meat on kitchen paper and season with pepper.

3. Pour the olive oil into the browning dish and (using tongs and wearing oven gloves) immediately add the meat. Turn it in the hot oil, 10 seconds at a time, on 3 or 4 sides to begin the browning process.

4. Microwave, uncovered, on HIGH, allowing 6 minutes for each 450 g (1 lb) weight of beef. The timing (in this case 19½ minutes) gives a rose pink centre and a well browned edge. Turn the beef over halfway through the cooking time; pour off and reserve the excess fat and juices (which, if not removed, impair cooking efficiency).

Allow 5–6 minutes per 450 g (1 lb) for very rare to rare beef.
Allow 7–9 minutes per 450 g (1 lb) for moderately to well cooked beef.

5. Remove the beef from the microwave oven and leave it to stand, generously tented in foil, for 10 minutes. During this time a considerable rise in temperature may be monitored by a meat thermometer.

6. Add the vinegars and wine to the juices in the still-hot dish. Stir well to dislodge all fragments from the base. Microwave, uncovered, on HIGH for 5 minutes.

7. Mix the cornflour and stock together and pour into the hot liquid. Microwave, uncovered, on HIGH for a further minute, stirring from the edge towards the centre.

8. Uncover the beef and carefully pour the accumulated juices into the gravy, stirring well. (Use the juices poured off halfway in another recipe.) Add the chopped parsley at this stage or later if preferred.

9. Serve the beef in thin slices, each seasoned by its anchovy inserts, with some of the strong delicious gravy.

See photograph page 47

──── SERVING TIP ────
Serve with Wild Rice (page 75), Vegetable au Naturel (page 66) or Minted Sweet Potato Shreds (page 69).

GOODHUSBAND'S BOLOGNESE

Once you have made this magically straight-forward sauce I can guarantee that never again will you want to make it in a saucepan. The meat is here allowed to 'brown' unaided and its colour develops on standing. No extra oil is used to cook the ingredients other than the juices and fat from the meat itself. Shredded potato helps to thicken and absorb these juices and also to test when the sauce is completely ready. All in all, this Bolognese takes just under 20 minutes to cook, yet yields a worthy result. Use the variations described as bases for any number of excellent dishes; they make for good husbandry!

Serves 4

450 g (1 lb) good quality beef, minced
1 medium onion, 100 g (4 oz), skinned and chopped
2 cloves garlic, skinned and chopped
2 sticks celery, 100 g (4 oz), sliced
1 medium carrot, 100 g (4 oz), thinly sliced
100 g (4 oz) prepared chicken livers, chopped finely
15 cm (6 inch) length lemon peel, crushed
7.5 ml (1½ level tsp) dried oregano or marjoram
2 fresh bay leaves
90 ml (6 tbsp) tomato purée
2.5 ml (½ level tsp) cayenne pepper
225 ml (8 fl oz) chianti or similar red wine
small bouquet of fresh parsley and thyme sprigs
1 small potato, 75 g (3 oz), coarsely grated
5 ml (1 level tsp) salt
freshly ground black pepper
30 ml (2 level tbsp) thick cream

1. Put the minced beef into a large, shallow heat-proof dish, browning dish or casserole. Micro-wave, uncovered, on HIGH for 5 minutes, stirring from time to time.
2. With a draining spoon, lift out and reserve the meat, leaving about 45 ml (3 tbsp) of fat and juices in the dish.
3. Add the onion, garlic, celery, carrot, chicken livers and crushed lemon peel. Stir well. Micro-wave, uncovered, on HIGH for 3 minutes,

stirring halfway through the cooking time.
4. Return the cooked meat to the dish with the oregano, bay leaves, tomato purée, cayenne, wine, herb bouquet and the potato (freshly grated with a coarse grater or food processor). Stir the ingredients together well.
5. Cover with a lid and microwave on HIGH for 7 minutes or until the potato tastes fully cooked, the flavours have blended and a good sauce consistency is obtained.
6. Add salt and pepper and stir in the cream to blend. Use immediately or cool, refrigerate and use the following day, by which time the flavour strengthens somewhat.

Variations

Use the Bolognese sauce the following ways:
1. Serve with freshly cooked pasta, such as tagliatelle (page 17). (Serves 4–6)
2. Packed inside halved, pocketed pitta bread, with shredded lettuce and cucumber on top. (Serves 6–8)
3. As a substitute for the meats in the recipe for Twice Baked Potatoes (page 29).
4. Mixed well into Basmati Rice With Herbs (page 75) to become a hearty form of Herbed Beef Risotto. (Serves 4–6)
5. Layered with Kibbled Wheat Pilaf (page 76) and topped with mozzarella and Parmesan cheese, it becomes a Peasant Casserole. (Serves 6–8)
6. Layered with slices of Aubergine au Naturel (page 66) and topped with Smoky Cheese Sauce (page 85), it is Moussaka. (Serves 6–8)

STEAKS WITH OYSTER BUTTER AND RED WINE SAUCE

Canned oysters in brine provide a surprisingly good taste in the pounded butter and red wine sauce which accompanies these steaks. Live oysters could of course be used (though the cost of 1½ dozen fresh oysters would tempt me to serve them as a separate course, I confess). The adage against mixing red wine and oysters seems not to apply in this particular instance. Make sure that the steaks are at room temperature, not chilled, when they are cooked. Also, allow the full preheating time for the browning dish. If preferred, this dish may be served with the butter or sauce separately.

Serves 2

| two 225 g (8 oz) Angus sirloin steaks |
| freshly ground black pepper |

Oyster butter

| 225 g (8 oz) can of oysters in brine |
| 25 g (1 oz) unsalted butter |
| 30 ml (2 level tbsp) chopped fresh parsley |
| 15 g ($\frac{1}{2}$ oz) clarified butter |

Red wine sauce

| 15 ml (1 level tbsp) reserved oyster juices and brine |
| 30 ml (2 tbsp) Burgundy |
| 5 ml (1 tsp) rich soy sauce or fish soy sauce |
| 12 reserved perfect oysters |

1. Pat the steaks dry on absorbent kitchen paper. Season the meat well on both sides with the black pepper, pressing it well in. Leave to stand.
2. To make the oyster butter, strain the oysters, reserving 15 ml (1 level tbsp) of their juices and brine for the sauce. Keep 12 of the best shaped oysters for the red wine sauce.
3. Pound, mash or chop the remaining drained oysters with the unsalted butter and parsley to form a paste. Shape into a roll and put into the freezer to become firm.
4. Wipe or paint the clarified butter over the surface of a 25 cm (10 inch) uncovered browning dish. Preheat the browning dish to the maximum recommended by the manufacturer.
5. Using tongs, place the steaks quickly in the dish without removing it from the oven. Microwave on HIGH for 1 minute, uncovered.
6. Using tongs, turn the steaks over and microwave on HIGH, uncovered, for a further minute.
7. Transfer the steaks to a heated serving dish. Add to the browning dish the reserved oysters, juice and brine, red wine and soy sauce. Microwave on HIGH for 1 minute. Stir well to dislodge all fragments on the base, taking care not to damage the oysters. If the sauce seems too thin, microwave for a further 30 seconds on HIGH.
8. Spoon half the sauce over each steak and put oyster butter rounds on to each. Serve immediately.

BEEF CARBONNADE

Flemish carbonnade traditionally contains beef, onions, herbs and beer and is always served with potatoes. My quick version has basically similar ingredients, but includes an aromatic 'gremolata' (garlic, lovage and lemon zest) sprinkled over at serving time. I find steamed or puréed potatoes a suitable accompaniment, with a crisp chicory salad to follow.

Serves 4

| 550 g ($1\frac{1}{4}$ lb) chuck or topside steak, cut into pieces 1.25 cm ($\frac{1}{2}$ inch) thick |
| 15 ml (1 level tbsp) flour |
| 30 ml (2 tbsp) virgin olive oil |
| 1 onion, skinned and chopped |
| 4 juniper berries, crushed |
| 450 ml (15 fl oz) brown ale |
| 1 vegetable stock cube, crumbled |
| 350 g (12 oz) flat mushrooms, quartered |

Garnish

| 2 garlic cloves, skinned and chopped |
| 5 ml (1 level tsp) lemon rind, grated |
| 15 ml (1 level tbsp) fresh lovage or flat leaf parsley, chopped |

1. Preheat a 20 cm (8 inch) browning dish on HIGH in the microwave oven for 6 minutes.
2. Using a meat hammer, cutlet bat or rolling pin, beat the meat thoroughly and then slice into 1 cm ($\frac{1}{2}$ inch) fingers. Pierce each meat finger twice with a skewer and then toss in the flour.
3. Quickly add the olive oil to the heated browning dish and then the floured meat. Microwave on HIGH for 1 minute, stirring once.
4. Add the onion, juniper berries, brown ale and a stock cube to the meat and cover with a lid. Microwave on HIGH for 5 minutes or until boiling and then reduce to MEDIUM power (60%) and microwave for 35–40 minutes, depending on the tenderness of the meat. Stir twice during cooking time and check that the meat is covered by liquid or it will discolour.
5. Remove the lid, stir in the mushrooms and microwave on HIGH, uncovered, for a further 4 minutes, stirring once.
6. Serve sprinkled with the garnish of garlic, lemon rind and lovage or parsley.

MINTED LAMB CHOPS ANGOSTURA

Using a microwave oven, in under 8 minutes you can have lamb chops cooked to pink perfection and create a sophisticated sauce to accompany them. If you prefer your lamb very well cooked, adjust the time accordingly. Serve with green beans and baby jacket potatoes.

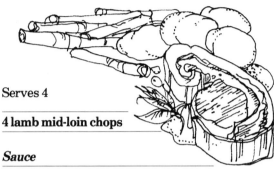

Serves 4

4 lamb mid-loin chops

Sauce

5 ml (1 tsp) Angostura bitters

25 g (1 oz) butter

60 ml (4 level tbsp) chopped fresh mint

salt and freshly ground black pepper

Garnish

4 fresh mint sprigs

1. Preheat a 25 cm (10 inch) browning dish for $3\frac{1}{2}$–4 minutes, or according to the manufacturer's instructions. Microwave the chops, uncovered, on HIGH for $2\frac{1}{2}$ minutes, turning with tongs (to avoid burning your hands) after 1 minute.
2. Pour off the fat from the pan and push the chops to one side.
3. Pour the Angostura bitters into the still-hot pan, stirring to dislodge the particles on the base, add butter and stir to blend. Add the mint and season, adjusting to taste.
4. Serve the chops with a little sauce poured over each and garnish with a fresh mint sprig.

SEASONED RACK OF LAMB WITH COURGETTES

A contrast of styles unites traditional and old-fashioned seasoning salt (best made in a mortar and pestle) and up-to-date pan roasting in the microwave oven. The initial browning seals and darkens the scored skin, while the meat inside cooks to a delicate pink. The courgettes in the seasoned juices and wine taste superb, especially with a fresh young Beaujolais-Villages or Médoc.

Serves 2–3

Seasoning

5 ml (1 level tsp) mild paprika

2.5 ml ($\frac{1}{2}$ level tsp) celery salt

2.5 ml ($\frac{1}{2}$ level tsp) ground bay leaves

2.5 ml ($\frac{1}{2}$ level tsp) onion salt

2.5 ml ($\frac{1}{2}$ level tsp) dried marjoram

2 allspice berries

8 white peppercorns

550 g ($1\frac{1}{4}$ lb) rack of lamb, chined

15 ml (1 tbsp) grapeseed oil

2 cloves garlic, roughly crushed

225 g (8 oz) courgettes, thinly sliced

30 ml (2 tbsp) white wine

1. Using a pestle and mortar, pound all the seasoning ingredients to a powder. Score the surface skin and fat of the lamb diagonally at 1.25 cm ($\frac{1}{2}$ inch) intervals. Rub the seasoning salt into the scored surface and the fat.
2. Preheat a large 25 cm (10 inch) browning dish for 5 minutes on HIGH. Add the oil, then the lamb, scored surface down, and the crushed garlic cloves.
3. Microwave, uncovered, for 5–7 minutes on HIGH, turning the meat over and standing it upright after 2 minutes. Transfer the meat to a serving dish, cover and keep warm.
4. Add the courgettes and wine to the browning pan, stir to coat the courgettes, and microwave on HIGH for a further 2 minutes. Remove the garlic and discard.
5. Allow 2 or 3 sliced cutlets for each serving, with a share of courgettes in sauce.

LOIN OF LAMB WITH SALSIFY AND MUSHROOMS

Meats roasted for any period over 15 minutes in the microwave oven tend to brown naturally and to colour further once they are removed and left to stand. In this recipe, however, the mustard-honey-soy mixture browns richly and gives particular sweet flavour to a choice small lamb joint. Salsify (or scorzonera) is a vegetable of considerable merit and its 'oyster'-like taste makes a notable contribution to this dish.

Serves 4

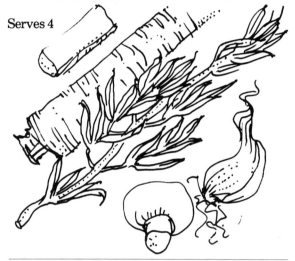

1 kg (2¼ lb) boned loin of lamb, scored
15 ml (1 level tbsp) dry mustard powder
15 ml (1 level tbsp) rosemary honey
15 ml (1 level tbsp) rich soy sauce
225 g (8 oz) button mushrooms, halved
225 g (8 oz) salsify, peeled
50 g (2 oz) shallots, skinned and sliced
15 ml (1 level tbsp) chopped fresh chervil
15 ml (1 level tbsp) fresh rosemary leaves
15 ml (1 level tbsp) mild Dijon mustard

1. Ask the butcher to score the fat of the meat in parallel lines or a criss-cross pattern before rolling and tying.
2. Rub the dry mustard well into the surface of the lamb. Mix together the honey and soy sauce and brush evenly over the prepared surface.
3. Put the meat in an oven bag and place it on a roasting rack. Pierce the bag in several places and secure, using a non-metallic tie, rubber band or string. Microwave on MEDIUM (60%) for 18–20 minutes. During cooking, pour off and reserve the accumulated juices. Give the rack a quarter turn every 4½–5 minutes.
4. Remove from the oven and tent with foil. Leave the meat to stand for 10–15 minutes, depending on how well done the lamb is preferred. (The shorter time will give a more rosy result.)
5. Put the reserved juices, about 50 ml (2 fl oz), into a measuring jug and cool quickly (by adding ice cubes to the juices or putting the jug into the freezer) for 15 minutes for the fat to solidify. It can then be easily separated from the cooking juices.
6. Halve the mushrooms crosswise. Halve the salsify lengthwise, then cut it crosswise into 5 cm (2 inch) lengths.
7. Put 25 g (1 oz) of the solidified fat into a large, shallow heatproof dish. Microwave, uncovered, on HIGH for 30 seconds or until it melts. Toss the salsify, mushrooms and shallots in the melted fat until they are well coated. Microwave, uncovered, on HIGH for 2 minutes.
8. Add the chopped chervil, rosemary and the reserved juices. Mix well, cover and microwave on HIGH for 8 minutes or until the salsify is tender but still firm.
9. Stir the Dijon mustard into the sauce and microwave, covered, on HIGH for 1 minute. Taste and adjust the seasonings.
10. Slice the meat thickly into medallions and serve with some sauce, surrounded by the vegetables.

See photograph page 47

——— **SERVING TIP** ———
A creamy vegetable such as Pumpkin Purée (page 68) would be an interesting accompaniment to this dish, followed by a green salad.

NECTARINE-STUFFED MEAT BALLS

Each of these large meatballs contains a pleasant surprise – nuggets of perfectly cooked nectarine. If nectarines are not available, substitute a fresh peeled peach or four presoaked dried apricots.

Serves 4

350 g (12 oz) lean lamb, twice minced
½ onion, skinned and chopped
15 ml (1 level tbsp) chopped fresh mint leaves
2.5 ml (½ level tsp) salt
5 ml (1 level tsp) rich soy sauce
4 fresh mint leaves, crushed
1 fresh nectarine, stoned and quartered

1. Add the lamb to the onion, mint, salt and soy sauce and then beat until thoroughly and smoothly blended.
2. Lightly oil 4 heatproof ramekins or 4 hollows of a microware bun dish. Place a crushed mint leaf on the base of each.
3. Spoon a quarter of the mixture into each hollow. Using a finger or wooden spoon handle, make a deep hole in the meat. Dice the nectarine quarters and use them to fill the holes, pressing the fruit in firmly. Spread the meat back over the filling to enclose the fruit and pat firmly into place.
4. Microwave, uncovered, on HIGH for 5 minutes, rotating the bun pan or rearranging the ramekins halfway through cooking time. Allow to stand for 2–3 minutes. (The surface darkens on standing as the meat continues to cook.)
5. Serve the meat balls cut into halves, or quarters, to show the fruited interior. Pour the cooking juices over, or reserve them for making Saffron Cream Sauce (see page 79).

ROAST LAMB RUZZOLATA

Cured beef (Bünderfleisch or Bresaola), sliced paper-thin with fresh basil rolled cigar-like inside it, is inserted into this (otherwise classic) microwaved roast leg of lamb. The inserts give a medieval look, while the thickish slices of rosy lamb reveal ruby-red circles of beef set into their circumference. The accompanying sauce, enriched with egg yolk, provides a mellow finish to this superb dish. The basic timing and necessary techniques for cooking lamb on the bone are shown below. The meat must be at room temperature and well dried before cooking begins.

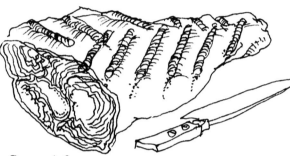

Serves 4–6

12 thin slices, 50 g (2 oz) Bünderfleisch or Bresaola
12 fresh basil leaves
2 kg (4½ lb) leg of English lamb
freshly ground black pepper
50 ml (2 fl oz) Amarone or similar red wine
15 ml (1 tbsp) rich soy sauce
1 egg yolk, at room temperature

Garnish (optional)

fresh bay leaves

1. On each slice of beef, place one basil leaf and roll both up tightly so that each 'cigar' totally encloses its leaf. (Each 'cigar' should be the width of a pencil.)
2. Placing the lamb fleshiest side upwards, use a sharp knife to make 6 diagonal slashes, about 7.5 cm (3 inch) long, in a herringbone pattern on the two sloping top surfaces. Push a beef and basil 'cigar' into each cut, so that the 12 insets are at the same surface level as the rest of the lamb. Season well with freshly ground black pepper.
3. Put the lamb on a heatproof microware

roasting rack or dish and microwave, uncovered, on HIGH. The timing (in this case 27 minutes) gives a deep pink to rosy colour at the bone, with a delicately well browned edge. Give the lamb a half turn halfway through cooking time, pouring off all juices and fat collected in the roasting dish into a small heatproof sauceboat.

Allow 5–6 minutes per 450 g (1 lb) for very rare pink lamb.
Allow 7–8 minutes per 450 g (1 lb) for medium to well cooked lamb.

4. At the end of cooking time, remove the lamb from the microwave oven and leave it to stand, generously tented in foil, for 10 minutes. During this time a considerable rise in temperature may be monitored by a meat thermometer.
5. Scrape all the debris from the roasting dish into the sauceboat. Add the red wine and soy sauce, then taste, adding pepper if necessary. Stir well. Microwave, uncovered, on HIGH for 2 minutes or until hot.
6. In a separate heatproof small bowl or cup, stir the egg yolk with 2 tablespoons of the hot sauce. Return this mixture to the sauceboat and microwave on HIGH for 30–40 seconds, stirring from the edges to the centre at 10 second intervals.
7. Slice the lamb into thick wedges, each containing some of the beef. Pour any juices from the lamb into the sauceboat and serve with the meat, garnished with basil if wished.

—— **COOK'S TIP** ——
If no fresh basil is available, fresh marjoram or oregano can be used instead. Though good, the result will not of course be the same.

PORK BROCHETTES WITH PEANUT SAUCE

Microwave cooking emphasises the fragrant flavours of this dish and keeps the meat tender and succulent. The amount of chilli given here can be varied, depending on your own personal taste. Similarly, use smooth or crunchy peanut butter for the texture you prefer. Accompany with wild rice (see page 75) or plain steamed rice.

Serves 4

550 g (1¼ lb) pork fillet

Marinade

5 ml (1 level tsp) five-spice powder

2.5–5 ml (½–1 level tsp) hot chilli powder

1 shallot, sliced

75 ml (5 tbsp) light soy sauce

Sauce

90 ml (6 level tbsp) peanut butter

15 ml (1 tbsp) rich soy sauce

juice of 1½ fresh limes

To serve

½ head curly endive or cos lettuce, torn or shredded, or Batavian endive

15 ml (1 level tbsp) chopped fresh coriander leaves

½ fresh lime, sliced

1. Slice the pork fillet crosswise into ten pieces, then cut each slice crosswise in half. Thread the pork evenly onto four bamboo satay sticks or fine wooden skewers.
2. Mix the marinade ingredients and pour over the meat in a shallow heatproof dish. Leave to marinate for 1 hour, turning the meat several times. Drain, reserving the marinade.
3. Position the skewers with their meat round the edges of the dish to form a square. Cover loosely with cling film. Microwave on HIGH for 8–10 minutes, basting halfway through cooking time and giving the dish a half turn. Set the meat aside.
4. To make the sauce, stir the peanut butter, rich soy sauce and lime juice into the marinade. Microwave on HIGH for 1 minute, stirring after 30 seconds.
5. Dress a serving dish with shredded lettuce and place the pork on top. Spoon sauce over the meat and scatter with coriander leaves. Garnish with twists of lime.

MANGO AND CHILLI TENDERLOIN

Mango gives delicious succulence to this faintly Thai-influenced pork dish. The taste of fresh limes and fish-flavoured chilli paste (both available from Thai food stores or Asian supermarkets) gives a certain vividness to an already fragrant marinade-cum-sauce. The technique described, of cutting mango accurately to give neat cubes and without undue waste, takes some effort but is worth learning, as is the method for preparing the pork to give double portion medallions.

Serves 4

3 ripe, medium mangoes, 700 g (1½ lb)

550 g (1¼ lb) pork tenderloin fillet

15 ml (1 tbsp) grapeseed oil

juice of 1 lime

7.5 ml (1½ level tsp) Namprik Narok chilli paste

50 ml (2 fl oz) chicken stock

5 ml (1 level tsp) salt

freshly ground black pepper

Garnish (optional)

fresh flat leaf parsley or coriander leaves

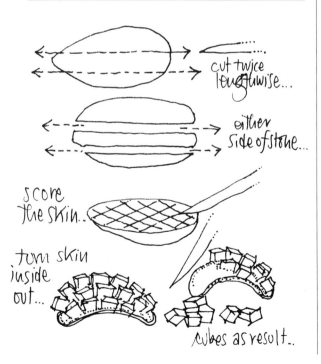

1. Slice each mango twice lengthwise (either side of the stone) then scrape away and reserve the flesh from the stone sections. Using a spoon, scoop out the flesh from the 2 mango slices, then score and turn the skins of the other 4 mango slices inside out. Slice off and remove the mango flesh in neat cubes. Purée the scooped out flesh using a food processor or blender, keeping the cubes aside.
2. Slice the pork fillet into 2.5 cm (1 inch) 'medallions' and slice each medallion almost in half again, but without cutting right through. Open out to give a larger 'figure of 8' shape. Use a meat hammer or rolling pin to flatten each piece between 2 sheets of cling film.
3. Put the pork pieces and oil into a large, shallow, heatproof dish, such as a 25 cm (10 inch) browning dish. Sprinkle with lime juice and chilli paste and cover with the puréed mango. Loosely cover with cling film and leave to marinate for 20 minutes.
4. Add the chicken stock to the pork and mango and microwave, loosely covered, on HIGH for 8 minutes, stirring halfway through the cooking time.
5. Stir in the cubed mango flesh and microwave, uncovered, on HIGH for a further 5 minutes.
6. Season to taste with salt and freshly ground black pepper, and garnish with the flat leaf parsley or coriander leaves if wished.

LUGANIGA WITH MUSTARD AND PEPPER SAUCE

Luganiga is an Italian coiled pure pork sausage, usually coarsely chopped, with pepper and seasonings added. It normally weighs a little over 450 g (1 lb). A thicker version called Napoli is sometimes available, also from specialist delicatessens. The well-known Cumberland sausage is a perfectly acceptable and more frequently available substitute. In this recipe the delicious juices contribute to a tasty peppery sauce. The dish would be perfect served with a bowl of creamy celeriac, turnip or carrot purée and cabbage with caraway seeds. A glass of Chianti, Barbera or Soave would give added pleasure.

Serves 4

40 g (1½ oz) unsalted butter

450 g (1 lb) Luganiga or Napoli coiled pork sausage

30 ml (2 level tbsp) Dijon mustard, hot

60 ml (4 tbsp) red wine, such as Chianti or Barbera

15 ml (1 level tbsp) green peppercorns in brine, drained and crushed

1 garlic clove, skinned and chopped

Garnish

60 ml (4 tbsp) chopped fresh parsley

1. Preheat a 25 cm (10 inch) browning dish for the maximum time recommended by the manufacturer. Take 15 ml (1 level tbsp) unsalted butter and rub a little over one surface of the coiled sausage. Add what remains of this butter to the hot pan, without removing it from the microwave oven.
2. Add the sausage and microwave, uncovered, on HIGH for 2 minutes. Using a fish slice, turn the sausage over in one neat movement. Microwave, uncovered, for a further 2 minutes on HIGH. Test the sausage for firmness but be sure not to puncture the skin.
3. Moving the sausage to one corner of the dish, add the mustard, wine, the remaining 25 g (1 oz) butter, peppercorns and garlic clove, stirring to blend them. Microwave, uncovered, on HIGH for 2 minutes, giving the dish a half turn twice during the final cooking period. Shake the pan well to distribute the sauce evenly.
4. Serve sprinkled with parsley.

VEAL MEDALLIONS WITH JUNIPER

Delicious little mouthfuls of veal with 'clouds' of mushroom on top combine with a lively sauce to make an excellent supper or lunch dish. The veal must be sliced fairly thickly; thin slices cooked by this method would be unappetisingly dry and tough. Cloud ear fungus, which is to be found in Asian food stores, quickly triples in size when soaked in hot water and becomes deliciously tender.

Serves 4

8 dried cloud ear mushrooms

450 g (1 lb) fillet of veal

roughly crushed black peppercorns

15 g (½ oz) butter

12 juniper berries, crushed

15 ml (1 level tbsp) grated lemon rind

5 ml (1 tsp) lemon juice

45 ml (3 tbsp) medium sherry

30 ml (2 tbsp) double cream

Garnish (optional)

lemon slices

1. Soak the cloud ear mushrooms in 150 ml (¼ pint) hot water. Preheat a 25 cm (10 inch) browning dish on HIGH for 7 minutes, or according to the manufacturer's instructions.
2. Slice the veal into 8 even-sized chunks or 'medallions' and season with freshly ground black pepper.
3. Put the butter in the preheated browning dish and quickly add the pieces of meat, turning them in the butter to brown on each side. Add the crushed juniper berries, lemon rind, lemon juice, sherry and cream. Stir well and microwave, uncovered, on HIGH for 4 minutes, stirring and turning the meat halfway through cooking time. Top each piece of veal with one cloud ear mushroom, and spoon sauce over and around each serving. Garnish with twists of lemon.

See photograph page 48

———— **SERVING TIP** ————
Mange-tout peas or French beans would make a fine accompaniment to this dish.

V·E·G·E·T·A·B·L·E·S A·N·D G·R·A·I·N·S

VEGETABLES AU NATUREL

Many vegetables grow naturally 'packaged' in their own sturdy leaves, skins or pods. Exploit this quality by microwaving such vegetables intact, so the food cooks in all its own juices. To prevent bursting it is important to pierce the surface of the vegetable in several places. Then place it in the microwave oven, on greaseproof or absorbent kitchen paper, a heatproof plate or container. Vegetables particularly suited to this type of cooking are potatoes, sweet corn on the cob, aubergines, tomatoes and carrots.

POTATOES

One of the simplest, most comforting, foods in the world is the humble potato. It has no crusty skin when cooked in a microwave oven, but I always find that when cooked like this, potatoes tend to be eaten to the last scrap of skin, so tasty are they!

Serves 4

---

four 175 g (6 oz) potatoes, scrubbed

15 ml (1 level tbsp) chopped fresh chives, parsley, dill, mint or basil

50 g (2 oz) quark, fromage blanc, unsalted butter or clotted cream

freshly ground sea salt and black pepper

---

1. Pierce the potatoes with a fork twice on both sides. Place in the microwave oven, arranged in a circle on a square of absorbent kitchen paper, and microwave on HIGH for 10–12 minutes, turning the potatoes over and rearranging their positions once.
2. Wrap in foil and leave to stand for 5 minutes.
3. Cross-cut the potato diagonally and push upwards to expose the cooked potato flesh. Add the herb or herb mixture of your choice and a portion of the cheese, butter or cream to each, seasoning well.

AUBERGINES

Remember the time it used to take to bake an aubergine in a conventional oven? Aubergine cooked this way is child's play and tastes delicious. Even more fascinating is that the aubergine flesh is really pale green, not boring brown, when cooked by perfect techniques. These silky slices falling softly from the knife are a sight to behold.

Serves 4

---

350 g (12 oz) large aubergine with stem intact

2.5 ml ($\frac{1}{2}$ tsp) olive oil

Dressing

150 ml ($\frac{1}{4}$ pint) natural yogurt

1.25 ml ($\frac{1}{4}$ tsp) ground ginger

1.25 ml ($\frac{1}{4}$ tsp) ground cumin

30 ml (2 level tbsp) chopped fresh mint

freshly ground salt and black pepper

---

1. Wipe the surface of the aubergine and dry well on absorbent kitchen paper. Rub with the olive oil. Pierce 6 times down each side with a fork. Place on absorbent kitchen paper and microwave on HIGH for 6 minutes, turning over halfway through the cooking time.
2. Remove from the oven and allow to stand for 2 minutes.
3. Mix together the yogurt, ginger, cumin and mint, seasoning to taste.
4. Carefully cut the aubergine into 12 slices and cover with the dressing. Alternatively, use the cooked vegetable to make Aubergine Dip Clara (page 87).

TOMATOES

What could be simpler than this recipe? Yet the fresh sweet taste is always a surprise. The cooked tomatoes can accompany meat, fish, rice, barley or kibbled wheat; be stuffed and eaten as a warm salad; mashed with a fork on toast or warm rolls; and, with added anchovies, blue cheese dressing or cottage cheese, become a quick snack. Put into a blender with a little butter and white wine or orange juice and you have the healthiest tomato soup ever invented.

Serves 4

4 medium beefsteak tomatoes

salt and freshly ground pepper

5 ml (1 level tsp) butter

5 ml (1 level tsp) fresh oregano, chopped

1. Wash the tomatoes and wipe dry. Place the stem end downwards on opposite sides of a heat-proof plate and make three deep intersecting cross-cuts in each tomato.
2. Microwave on HIGH for 3–4 minutes, giving the dish a half turn halfway through cooking time. Leave to stand for 2 minutes.
3. To serve, widen the cross-cuts, smooth back any loose inner flesh, season and add a portion of butter and fresh oregano to each.

CORN ON THE COB

Some people believe that sweet corn, when cooked by this method, barely needs butter, salt or pepper, it tastes so fresh. Certainly it has wonderful firm sweetness but I still enjoy my butter and seasonings, as indicated below.

Serves 4

4 freshly picked cobs (with silk and green husk intact)

water for washing

50 g (2 oz) butter, in 4 portions (optional)

salt and freshly ground pepper (optional)

1. Rinse the whole cobs in cold water, without shaking dry. Arrange them, radiating outwards, on absorbent kitchen paper. Microwave on HIGH for 8–9 minutes, depending on size, turning the cobs over and rearranging their positions once.
2. Wrap in foil and leave to stand for 2 minutes. Pull open the husks and silk to expose the kernels. Add a portion of butter and, seasonings, if wished.

——————— COOK'S TIP ———————
As an alternative, in place of butter one of the following dips or sauces may be used:
Creamy garlic pasta sauce (page 85)
Creamy lovage and orange herb dip (page 87)
Fresh tomato sauce (page 80)
Fruited fresh tomato sauce (page 80)
Pimento coulis (page 77)
Sauce hollandaise and variations (page 79)
Sauce sancerre (page 77)

CARROTS

These slices have the long-cooked, old-fashioned taste normally associated with carrots in a pot roast or soup. Yet they are cooked in under 5 minutes! Slicing them thinly for serving can be fascinating: soft, tender insides lie beneath a skin firm enough to 'pop' with crispness when bitten into. I find it hard to cook carrots in conventional ways, now I have discovered their true taste.

Serves 4

225 g (8 oz) whole carrots, scrubbed, topped and tailed

Dressing

freshly ground salt and pepper

60 ml (4 tbsp) single cream or soured cream

5 ml (1 level tsp) fresh dill

1. Pierce the carrots in 5 or 6 places evenly down their length. Arrange them on a sheet of absorbent kitchen paper, greaseproof paper or a heatproof plate.
2. Microwave on HIGH for 4 minutes, turning the carrots halfway through cooking time. Leave to stand for 2 minutes.
3. Hold the carrots in kitchen paper and slice very thinly. Season, add the dressing ingredients and serve hot or cold.

EARLY AUTUMN PUMPKIN PURÉE

When cooked in a microwave oven, pumpkin seems to retain a particular nutty sweetness. Even the most bigoted vegetable-haters will love this mixture, which is stunning to look at and indecently delicious in flavour. Dill was flowering in my tiny garden when I first prepared this dish, so I celebrated by using it as a decorative and tasty garnish. Fennel or parsley flower heads could be used instead.

Serves 4

450 g (1 lb) pumpkin, skinned and cubed

30 ml (2 tbsp) water

salt and freshly ground black pepper

30 ml (2 tbsp) single cream

2.5 ml (½ level tsp) grated nutmeg

Garnish

dill flowers

1. Put the pumpkin and water into a ring microwave mould. Cover with cling film and microwave on HIGH for 10 minutes, rotating the dish after 5 minutes.
2. Drain the pumpkin and purée briefly in a food processor, using short bursts to blend the salt, freshly ground black pepper, cream and nutmeg; or mash using a potato masher.
3. Spoon into a warmed serving dish and decorate with dill flowers.

HARLEQUIN CAPSICUMS EN PAPILLOTE

The three colours of peppers used here provide the sweetest tastes and brightest colours. Do not be tempted to substitute green peppers, as to my mind they give not at all the same result. If new black peppers are not available, confine the choice to red and yellow.

Serves 4

450 g (1 lb) mixed red, yellow and black sweet peppers

Dressing

45 ml (3 tbsp) virgin olive oil

15 ml (1 level tbsp) chopped fresh coriander leaves

freshly ground sea salt and freshly ground black pepper

1. Remove and discard stems, seeds and membrane from the peppers. Slice each pepper

crosswise into 0.5 cm ($\frac{1}{4}$ inch) rings.

2. Using one sheet of greaseproof paper or baking parchment about 25 cm × 20 cm (10 × 8 inches) place 6–8 rings of alternate colours along the centre. Fold the edges tidily but firmly to make a secure parcel. Repeat 3 times using the remaining slices.

3. Arrange the papillotes (paper parcels) evenly in the microwave oven and microwave on HIGH for 4 minutes, rearranging the positions halfway through cooking time.

4. In 4 tiny bowls put some of the olive oil, coriander and seasoning mixture. Place an unwrapped parcel on to each of the 4 serving plates (each with its little bowl of dressing).

5. Diners unwrap the parcel and dip each hot ring into their share of oil dressing. The combination of colours, sweetness and herbal fragrance will give much pleasure.

See photograph page 82

MINTED SWEET POTATO SHREDS

Everyone, from the most choosy toddlers to hard-to-please gourmet octogenarians, will be amazed by this recipe. A food processor makes the preparation effortless, and the whole dish from start to serving time will take 10 minutes. But the real bonus is the delicacy of the melting sweet shreds in the mouth – quite superb, I think. Mint and a touch of brown sugar add the final flourish.

Serves 4

450 g (1 lb) sweet potato, coarsely grated

45 ml (3 tbsp) water

45 ml (3 level tbsp) butter

10 ml (2 level tsp) chopped fresh mint

5 ml (1 level tsp) soft dark brown sugar

1. Put the grated sweet potato and water into a large, heatproof bowl, cover with cling film and microwave on HIGH for 5 minutes.

2. Drain the potato and stir in the butter and chopped mint.

3. Serve immediately, sprinkled with the brown sugar.

MANGE-TOUT IN GARLIC DRESSING

The names mange-tout, snow peas or asparagus peas (as they are known in various countries) seem to me as charming as the objects themselves. Freshly green, succulent and wholly edible, they can be served many ways. The important thing is to retain their 'crunchiness'. In this recipe a powerful dressing emphasises their delicate taste and the combination of cold and hot is most intriguing. They remain delicious served cold, as the garlic dressing intensifies in flavour.

Serves 2–4

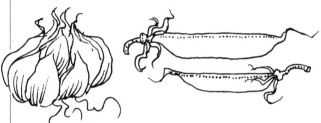

225 g (8 oz) mange-tout, topped and washed but not dried

15 g ($\frac{1}{2}$ oz) butter

salt and freshly ground black pepper

Dressing

150 ml ($\frac{1}{4}$ pint) soured cream

2 garlic cloves, skinned and crushed

pinch cayenne pepper

1. Put the mange-tout, butter, salt and pepper into a shallow, heatproof dish. Cover with cling film and microwave on HIGH for 2 minutes. Remove the cling film.

2. To make the dressing, combine the soured cream and garlic thoroughly and pour over the mange-tout. Sprinkle with pepper to garnish.

See photograph page 82

ONION PETALS WITH MUSTARD BUTTER

Although onions can be cooked whole, like jacket potatoes, this recipe is novel in that the quartered onions, curved sides downwards, retain their shape perfectly and seem to grow even more delectably sweet without losing any of their earthy appeal. Because they are cooked on the same plate as they are served, and need no stirring, the pattern of segments radiating outwards makes the 'petals' look more like part of a flower.

Serves 4

275 g (10 oz) large Spanish onions, skinned and quartered

10 ml (2 level tsp) mustard seeds, crushed

25 g (1 oz) butter, softened

Garnish
flat leaf parsley sprigs

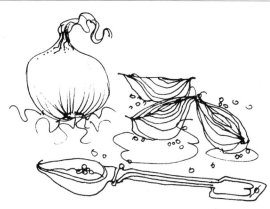

1. Place the onion quarters curved side downwards on a heat-proof serving plate and arrange in a pattern radiating outwards, like petals of a flower. (If the onions are very large, cut them into 8 segments.)
2. Mix the mustard seeds together with the softened butter and spread this mixture over the onions.
3. Cover with cling film and microwave on HIGH for 6 minutes.
4. Garnish with parsley and serve immediately.

See photograph page 84

GLAZED BABY ONIONS

Mixtures containing butter and sugar attract heat in a microwave oven, so the onions in this recipe cook perfectly in a deliciously buttery spiced sauce. The sesame seeds provide an unusual taste and texture contrast.

Serves 4

225 g (8 oz) baby onions, skinned

15 g (½ oz) butter

10 ml (2 level tsp) caster sugar

1.25 ml (¼ tsp) ground cumin

freshly ground black pepper

5 ml (1 level tsp) toasted sesame seeds

salt

Garnish (optional)
fresh coriander leaves

1. Place the onions, butter, sugar, ground cumin and black pepper on a shallow, heatproof casserole dish.
2. Cover with a lid and microwave on HIGH for 5 minutes, stirring once halfway through cooking time.
3. Serve the onions in their sauce, sprinkled with the poppy seeds, add salt to taste and garnish with the coriander leaves.

――――― **SERVING TIP** ―――――
Cheese biscuits or wafers spread with curd cheese can be served with the onions as a course on their own.

SPICED QUILTED POTATOES

This novel way of exposing the potato flesh means that it cooks more evenly and quickly. The tawny spiced mixture forms a pleasant semi-crisp crust and gives extra flavour.

Serves 4

four 100 g (4 oz) potatoes, scrubbed and halved crosswise

Seasoning

15 ml (1 level tbsp) soft brown sugar

2.5 ml ($\frac{1}{2}$ level tsp) garlic salt

0.6 ml ($\frac{1}{8}$ level tsp) ground cinnamon

Garnish (optional)

Smetana or buttermilk

1. Make deep diagonal slashes, almost to the skin, in the cut side of each potato half at 1 cm ($\frac{1}{2}$ inch) intervals. Cut crosswise in similar fashion to give a quilted effect. Rub or sprinkle the dry ingredients evenly over the cut surfaces.
2. Place, cut sides uppermost, around the edges of a heatproof plate and microwave, uncovered, on HIGH for 10–12 minutes. Turn the outer ends of each potato towards the centre halfway through cooking time. Eat hot with a trickle of buttermilk if wished.

GOLDEN FRIED POTATO CUBES

Though potatoes cooked this way are less crunchy than conventionally-cooked, sautéed potato cubes would be, their glowing colour is pleasing and they taste very wholesome. If a bacon, gherkin and sweet-sour dressing is made, they form the basis of a very good potato salad.

Serves 4

450 g (1 lb) potatoes, scrubbed and cubed

15 ml (1 level tbsp) flour

2.5 ml ($\frac{1}{2}$ level tsp) paprika

2.5 ml ($\frac{1}{2}$ level tsp) turmeric

5 ml (1 level tsp) celery salt

freshly ground black pepper

30 ml (2 tbsp) sunflower seed oil

Garnish (optional)

celery leaves

1. Preheat a large 25 cm (10 inch) browning dish for 6–8 minutes, following the manufacturer's instructions.
2. Put the potatoes into a plastic bag containing the flour, spices and seasonings. Inflate the bag and shake until the potatoes are well coated.
3. Put the oil into the browning dish and quickly add the potatoes, tossing to coat them in oil.
4. Microwave, uncovered, on HIGH for 3 minutes, then stir the potatoes, cover and microwave on HIGH for 2–3 minutes longer.
5. Drain and serve, with a celery leaf garnish if wished.

ITALIAN-STYLE TOMATOES

The perfect symmetry of plum tomatoes (as opposed to the chaotically disordered shapes of the larger French beefsteak or Marmande variety) has always pleased me. Their flavour, too, is special, as is the scent of fresh basil. Make the most of these tomatoes by cooking them minimally and serving with hot herb bread (page 19) for a snack or meal at any time of the day.

Serves 4

450 g (1 lb) plum tomatoes, washed and sliced into 1 cm ($\frac{1}{2}$ inch) rounds

$\frac{1}{4}$–$\frac{1}{2}$ chilli, seeded and thinly sliced

15 ml (1 level tbsp) chopped onion

15 ml (1 level tbsp) chopped fresh basil leaves

15 ml (1 tbsp) fruity olive oil

2.5 ml ($\frac{1}{2}$ level tsp) sugar

1. Put the tomatoes into a shallow casserole dish and add layers of the remaining ingredients in order.
2. Cover and microwave on HIGH for 3 minutes, turning the dish halfway through the cooking time.
3. Serve immediately with bread to soak up the juices.

SPICED AND BUTTERED COURGETTES

When covering vegetables with cling film in order to cook them quickly, it is often necessary to stir them part-way through cooking. To facilitate this process, and avoid burning your hands, leave a tiny gap at the edge of the firmly-stretched cling film in which to insert the wooden spoon for stirring.

Serves 4

450 g (1 lb) small courgettes, quartered crosswise then lengthwise

2 garlic cloves, skinned and chopped

25 g (1 oz) butter, cubed

7.5 ml (1½ level tsp) coriander seeds, well crushed

salt and pepper

1. Put the courgettes, garlic, butter and coriander seeds in a heatproof, shallow serving dish, cover with cling film and microwave on HIGH for 5 minutes. Give the dish a half turn and stir gently halfway through cooking time.
2. Season to taste and serve the courgettes in their spiced butter sauce, hot or warm.

MUSHROOMS WITH CREAM AND COGNAC

Cognac, cream and fresh lovage transform mushrooms into a feast. Use the increasingly available oyster mushrooms for a more delicately textured dish, but ordinary cultivated mushrooms also work well. Serve with buttered croûtes, crusty French bread or rye bread. These quantities serve two as a main course or four as a starter.

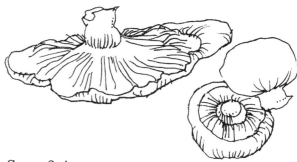

Serves 2–4

175 g (6 oz) oyster or button mushrooms

25 g (1 oz) butter, cut into cubes

15 ml (1 level tbsp) Cognac

5 ml (1 level tsp) chopped lovage leaves

60 ml (4 tbsp) double cream

salt and freshly ground black pepper

1. If the oyster mushrooms have stems, remove them and slice to the same thickness as the mushroom caps. Halve or slice the button mushrooms if large.
2. Put the butter, mushrooms, Cognac and the chopped herbs in a shallow heatproof dish, cover with a lid and microwave on HIGH for 3 minutes. Turn the mushrooms over halfway through the cooking time.
3. Transfer the mushrooms, using a slotted spoon, to a heated serving dish and keep warm.
4. Stir the cream into the buttery juices and microwave, uncovered, on HIGH for a further 45 seconds. Season with salt and pepper to taste.
5. Pour the sauce over the mushrooms and serve hot.

—— COOK'S TIP ——
If lovage is unavailable, flat leaf parsley may be used instead, though the flavour will not be as 'special'.

CAULIFLOWER WITH ROSY DRESSING

I have found that the kind of ring dish more usually associated with cakes is also useful for cooking vegetables. They cook more evenly, and a brisk shake or rotation of the dish has the same effect as stirring, but damages the pieces less and saves effort. The purchased powdered Tandoori mix, available at most supermarkets, gives an unusual taste and pretty colour to the sauce. This is an excellent 10-minute luncheon dish, starter or vegetable accompaniment.

Serves 4

450 g (1 lb) cauliflower florets
60 ml (4 tbsp) water
1.25 ml ($\frac{1}{4}$ level tsp) salt
freshly ground black pepper
30 ml (2 tbsp) soured cream
120 ml (8 level tbsp) mayonnaise
2.5 ml ($\frac{1}{2}$ level tsp) Tandoori mix
5 ml (1 tsp) lime juice or lime cordial
1 spring onion, trimmed and chopped

1. Put the cauliflower and water into a ring dish. Cover and microwave on HIGH for 8 minutes, briskly shaking or rotating the dish once or twice. Season with salt and freshly ground black pepper and then set aside.
2. To make the dressing, combine the soured cream, mayonnaise, Tandoori mix, lime juice and onion. Pour this sauce over the cauliflower and shake or rotate again to coat evenly.

See photograph page 84

—— **SERVING TIP** ——
Serve either as a hot salad, allowing the warmth of the vegetables to heat the sauce, or chilled on a bed of chicory, lettuce or curly endive.

GREEN BEANS IN ONION DRESSING

Walking down London's Portobello Road market, a stone's throw from where I live, I am always entranced by the number and variety of green beans on offer. Bobby beans, scarlet runner beans, the more tender green runner beans, French beans and other Spanish and South African varieties are there for the choosing. But some care is needed in timing as their tenderness varies markedly. In this recipe walnut oil lends a mellow touch and adds something special to the dish. Serve as a vegetable or with brown bread and chilled Chablis as a starter.

Serves 4

450 g (1 lb) flat green runner beans, stringed and sliced diagonally into 1.25 cm ($\frac{1}{2}$ inch) pieces
45 ml (3 tbsp) water
1 small onion, chopped
15 ml (1 tbsp) walnut oil
2.5 ml ($\frac{1}{2}$ level tsp) salt
10 ml (2 level tsp) chopped fresh parsley

1. Put the beans and water into a shallow casserole dish. Cover with a lid and microwave on HIGH for 9 minutes, stirring after 4 minutes.
2. Add the chopped onion and stir into the mixture. Cover and microwave on HIGH for a further $3\frac{1}{2}$–4 minutes, stirring once.
3. Add the walnut oil, season with the salt and sprinkle with the chopped parsley.

STEAMED SUMMER CABBAGE

Turn cabbage into a gourmet dish with traditional embellishments such as wine, butter and fennel seeds. Use its juices as a sauce and serve with hearty dishes such as Toulouse sausage, pork, gammon or bacon. Seasoning is best left to the end of cooking time.

Serves 4

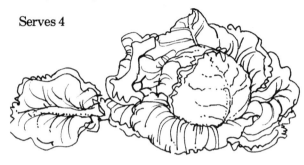

350 g (12 oz) summer cabbage, cored and cut into 4 wedges

15 ml (1 tbsp) dry white wine or dry cider

25 g (1 oz) butter

30 ml (2 tbsp) stock or water

2.5 ml ($\frac{1}{2}$ level tsp) fennel seeds

freshly ground sea salt

freshly ground black pepper

1. Put the cabbage, wine, butter, stock and fennel seeds in a shallow, heatproof casserole dish, cover with cling film and microwave on HIGH for $2\frac{1}{2}$ minutes.
2. Remove the cling film carefully (use cooking tongs to avoid burning your hands) and turn each cabbage portion over. Cover with new cling film and continue to microwave on HIGH for another $2\frac{1}{2}$ minutes.
3. Add salt and pepper to taste.

CARROT AND ORANGE JULIENNE

Although this elegant recipe is the perfect foil for many main course fish, game and poultry dishes, it is a pity not to serve it alone, occasionally, as a dish to be enjoyed for its own merits. The colours, shapes and overall prettiness make a pleasant change, and since no cooking liquid is lost, the vitamin value is enhanced. It makes a good dish for winter and summer alike.

Serves 4

350 g (12 oz) carrots, scraped and sliced into match-like strips

grated rind of 1 orange

15 ml (1 tbsp) water

25 g (1 oz) butter

flesh of 1 orange, segmented, pith removed

30 ml (2 level tbsp) chopped fresh coriander leaves

1. Put the carrots, orange rind, water and butter into a shallow dish. Cover with cling film and microwave on HIGH for 7 minutes.
2. Cut the orange segments crosswise into triangles and stir into the mixture. Cover with new cling film and microwave for 1 minute more on HIGH.
3. Add the freshly chopped coriander leaves and serve.

See photograph page 83

'SHOESTRING' CELERY WITH POPPY SEEDS

Celery prepared this way is a perfect partner for rich meat, poultry or game dishes as it retains a certain fresh and astringent taste. Cutting the stalks into 'shoestring'-length pieces may take time, but the end result is well worthwhile.

Serves 2–4

225 g (8 oz) celery, sliced into 5 cm (2 inch) 'shoestring' lengths

30 ml (2 tbsp) water

15 ml (1 tbsp) olive oil

30 ml (2 level tbsp) chopped fresh celery leaves

5 ml (1 level tsp) poppy seeds

1. Put the celery, water and olive oil into a shallow, heatproof dish. Cover and microwave on HIGH for 4 minutes.
2. Serve immediately, sprinkled with the celery leaves and poppy seeds.

BASMATI RICE WITH HERBS

Although rice cooks no faster in a microwave oven than by conventional cooking techniques, it tastes very good, needs no draining and can be served in the same bowl in which it is cooked. Dressed with fresh herbs, butter and aromatic vinegar, it gains new appeal. Rice vinegar is sold in most specialist Asian supermarkets.

Serves 4

225 g (8 oz) Basmati rice, washed and dried

2.5 ml ($\frac{1}{2}$ level tsp) salt

50 g (2 oz) butter

25 g (1 oz) mixed fresh herbs (parsley, chives, marjoram or thyme)

15 ml (1 tbsp) rice vinegar

1. Put the rice, 600 ml (1 pint) boiling water, salt and just 25 g (1 oz) of the butter into a large, deep, heatproof bowl and cover with cling film.
2. Microwave on HIGH for 10 minutes, turning the bowl once halfway through cooking time.
3. Leave to stand for a further 10 minutes, then remove the cling film and stir in the herbs, vinegar and the remaining 25 g (1 oz) butter.

―――――― **SERVING TIP** ――――――
Serve the rice hot, warm or cold as a salad or to accompany curries, casseroles, fricassees, spiced vegetables or vegetable purées.

WILD RICE

Expensive though it is to buy, and difficult to find, wild rice has a nutty texture and unique flavour which particularly complements game, fish and shellfish. Although the microwave oven saves little actual cooking time, wild rice cooked (after pre-soaking) by this method guarantees perfect results every time. Even better, it is good enough to be eaten on its own as a real indulgence!

Serves 4

100 g (4 oz) wild rice

1 garlic clove, skinned and chopped

15 ml (1 tbsp) fruity olive oil

2.5 ml ($\frac{1}{2}$ level tsp) sea salt

30 ml (2 level tbsp) chopped fresh chervil, chives, parsley or marjoram

1. Soak the rice in 600 ml (1 pint) warm water for about three hours. Drain through a sieve, discarding the water.
2. Put the rice, garlic, oil, salt and 600 ml (1 pint) boiling water into a medium deep, heatproof bowl or dish. Cover with cling film or a lid.
3. Microwave on HIGH for 30 minutes or until the rice is tender.
4. Allow to stand for 4–5 minutes.
5. Remove the cling film or lid and stir, adding the fresh herbs of your choice. Serve the rice hot, warm or cold.

BARLEY PEARLS

This rather neglected grain should be used more often. Microwave cooking seems to develop its mild taste and the grains grow plump and pleasantly tender; not soft, but merely cooked to an al dente firmness. Eaten hot as a vegetable accompaniment, or warm with the creamy dressing as a salad in its own right, it is well worth rediscovering. Use a fruit vinegar with a flavour you like – raspberry, strawberry, bramble or apple vinegars are some that come to mind.

Serves 4–6

225 g (8 oz) pearl barley
5 ml (1 level tsp) sea salt
15 g ($\frac{1}{2}$ oz) butter
4 blades mace
15 ml (1 tbsp) fruit vinegar

Dressing (optional)

60 ml (4 level tbsp) strained thick Greek yogurt
60 ml (4 level tbsp) mayonnaise
2 stalks celery, thinly sliced
25 g (1 oz) fresh mint, chopped

Garnish (optional)

mint sprigs

1. Cover the barley with some warm water to a depth of 5 cm (2 inches) in a deep heatproof bowl or casserole. Leave for 2 hours and then drain.
2. Add 150 ml ($\frac{1}{4}$ pint) fresh water, sea salt, butter and mace. Cover with cling film or a lid and microwave on HIGH for 10 minutes.
3. Leave to stand covered for a further 5 minutes. Drain off any remaining water and stir in the vinegar. Serve hot.
4. Alternatively, leave the dish to cool a little, then stir in the yogurt, mayonnaise, celery and chopped mint. Garnish, and eat as a starter, salad course or light lunch.

KIBBLED WHEAT PILAF

Kibbled wheat is sold in many health food stores and can make an unusual pilaf. As with many grains, soaking in advance softens the fibres, hastens cooking time, and reduces the amount of cooking water required. In this recipe the kibbled wheat can be soaked, cooked and served in the same dish. A generous use of fresh herbs is essential for this country dish, which is good enough to serve as a separate course accompanied by, say, Persian flat bread, unsalted butter and some good strong Cabernet or Zinfandel.

Serves 4

225 g (8 oz) kibbled wheat
25 g (1 oz) pine nuts
15 ml (1 tbsp) fruity olive oil
1 large onion, skinned and sliced
2 cloves garlic, skinned and chopped
30 ml (2 tbsp) water
5 ml (1 level tsp) sea salt
15 g ($\frac{1}{2}$ oz) unsalted butter
15 ml (1 level tbsp) fresh thyme leaves
30 ml (2 level tbsp) fresh parsley, chopped
5 ml (1 level tsp) fresh sage leaves, chopped
5 ml (1 level tsp) fresh rosemary leaves, chopped

1. Cover the kibbled wheat with some warm water to a depth of 5 cm (2 inches) in a 20 cm (8 inch) browning dish. Leave for $\frac{1}{2}$ hour, then drain in a sieve.
2. Put the pine nuts into the browning dish and microwave, uncovered, on HIGH for 3 minutes, stirring once. Add the oil, onion and garlic to the pan, stirring well. Microwave, uncovered, on HIGH for a further minute.
3. Add the drained kibbled wheat, the 30 ml (2 tbsp) water and sea salt to the browning pan. Stir, cover with a lid, and microwave on HIGH for 3 minutes, stirring from the sides to the centre once.
4. Stir the butter and herbs into the kibbled wheat, then cover and leave to stand for 3 minutes. Serve hot or cold.

S·A·U·C·E·S, D·I·P·S AND G·L·A·Z·E·S

PIMENTO COULIS

This stunning, strong-flavoured scarlet sauce will transform any food it accompanies. Avoid accidentally discarding the liquid from the pimento as it gives an essential contribution to the finished coulis. Using good quality processed peppers in liquid, rather than fresh peppers, is vital for this recipe. Serve the finished coulis hot with pan-grilled meat or fish, or with hot poultry, mousses, terrines or pâtés. Serve it cold as a 'mirror sauce' (see page 88) to coat the serving dish for cold meats. Make chilli-flavoured sherry by infusing whole fresh red chillies, stem end removed, in a similar volume of sherry. Seal loosely, stand in a warm place, shaking the jar occasionally, for one week. Strain, label and store.

Serves 4

1 jar pimentos (sweet red peppers), 280 g ($9\frac{7}{8}$ oz)

1 large garlic clove, skinned and chopped

15 ml (1 tbsp) Greek olive oil

75 ml (5 tbsp) liquid from pimento jar

5 ml (1 tsp) chilli-flavoured dry sherry or chilli vinegar (see above)

1.25 ml ($\frac{1}{4}$ level tsp) freshly ground black pepper

1. Drain the pimentos and chop. Reserve the liquid.
2. Using a food processor or blender, purée the pimento, garlic, oil and measured pimento liquid.
3. Add the remaining ingredients and microwave, covered, on HIGH for 2–3 minutes, stirring once.
4. For a thinner version, add 4 more tablespoons of pimento juice – and for an exceptionally smooth coulis or glaze, strain the sauce through a fine sieve.

See photograph page 82

SAUCE SANCERRE

A sharply fresh sauce this, as well suited to fresh vegetables as to white fish or shellfish. It can also be used warm as a dressing for smoked salmon, sturgeon, or to dress a salad containing the goat's cheeses called Chavignol.

Serves 4

50 g (2 oz) shallots, skinned and finely chopped

25 g (1 oz) butter

sprig of parsley

sprig of tarragon

sprig of chervil

250 ml (8 fl oz) Sancerre (or similar Loire wine)

Beurre manié

15 ml (1 level tbsp) butter

15 ml (1 level tbsp) flour

30 ml (2 tbsp) crème fraîche

1.25 ml ($\frac{1}{4}$ tsp) lemon pepper

5 ml (1 level tsp) fresh tarragon leaves, chopped

1. Put the shallots and butter into a small heat-proof bowl, cover and microwave on HIGH for $2\frac{1}{2}$ minutes.
2. Add the herb sprigs and wine. Cover and microwave on HIGH for 4 minutes.
3. Knead together the butter and flour to form beurre manié. Add this to the mixture in small pieces, stir in well and microwave, uncovered, on HIGH for 2 minutes, stirring once.
4. Add the crème fraîche, lemon pepper and fresh tarragon leaves. Serve hot, warm or cool.

SAUCE BOURGOGNE

The idea for this sauce comes from traditional 'Bourguignonne' recipes which use as their mainstay chunks of chicken or beef. Surprisingly, my light, new 'instant' version tastes as though it took far more time and skill to make than in reality. Serve over poached eggs, ham steaks, chops, grills, saucissons, steamed new potatoes or jacket potatoes. Delicious!

Serves 4

100 g (4 oz) rinded green bacon
10–12 button or pickling onions
1 fresh bay leaf, crushed
3 fresh sage leaves
1 small sprig fresh thyme
6–8 black peppercorns
90 ml (6 tbsp) beef or veal stock
90 ml (6 tbsp) red burgundy

Beurre manié

5 ml (1 level tsp) butter
5 ml (1 level tsp) flour

Garnish

15 ml (1 level tbsp) chopped fresh parsley

1. Cut the bacon into 1 cm (½ inch) cubes. Preheat a 20 cm (8 inch) browning dish on HIGH for 3½–4 minutes (or according to the manufacturer's instructions). Microwave the bacon and onions on HIGH for 2 minutes, covering loosely with two sheets of kitchen paper. Stir halfway through cooking time.
2. Add the herbs, peppercorns, stock and wine, cover with a lid and microwave on HIGH for a further 2 minutes.
3. Blend the butter and flour to a paste and add in small pieces to the sauce. Stir well, cover with a lid and microwave for a final 2 minutes, stirring halfway through cooking time. Serve sprinkled with parsley.

SAUCE MORILLE

Summon up any and all culinary excuses in order to make this delectable (but unfrugal) sauce. In our house it has been known to vanish completely before the pasta (with which it was to triumph) had finished cooking! If you keep a good store of basics, however, you can create more sauce at the touch of a microwave. Obviously, butter and cream are more convenient to locate than goose fat and crème fraîche, but when did inconvenience ever discourage a hedonist?

Serves 2–4

25 g (1 oz) dried morel or porcini mushrooms
300 ml (½ pint) warm water
25 g (1 oz) goose or duck fat or butter
1 garlic clove, skinned and chopped
8 green peppercorns in brine, drained and crushed
120 ml (8 tbsp) thick cream or crème fraîche
2.5 ml (½ level tsp) fine sea salt

1. Check that the stems and bases of the fungi are free from dried earth. Put the whole fungi into a medium heatproof bowl with the water and microwave on MEDIUM for 5 minutes, uncovered.
2. Put the fat (or butter) and garlic into a medium heatproof serving dish. Strain and remove all but four perfectly shaped fungi pieces from their cooking water. Shake them dry, chop and add to the fat-garlic mixture. Microwave on HIGH for 2 minutes, uncovered, stirring halfway through the cooking time.
3. Strain the fungi cooking liquid (discarding any grit) into the sauce and add the reserved fungi and the crushed green peppercorns. Microwave on HIGH, uncovered, for 10 minutes or until the volume is reduced by half, stirring halfway through cooking time.
4. Add the cream and salt and microwave on HIGH for 1 minute longer, to blend the flavours. Stir the thickened sauce gently and leave it to stand for 3–4 minutes, covered, to allow the full flavour to develop.

—————— **SERVING TIP** ——————
Sauce Morille is perfect with poached poultry, roasted game, grilled meats, sweetbreads, brains and pasta. Serve one perfect fungi with each portion of sauce.

SAUCE HOLLANDAISE

One of the great classics, this sauce seemed impossible to make successfully in a microwave oven. After several attempts we evolved a perfect method, but the instructions must be followed meticulously for absolute success. The warm, velvety smoothness of the sauce lends a voluptuousness to whatever it accompanies, from artichoke hearts to scallops.

Serves 4

3 egg yolks, size 2 (at room temperature)

30 ml (2 level tbsp) lemon juice

pinch of salt

pinch of white pepper

100 g (4 oz) butter (at room temperature)

1. Put the egg yolks, lemon juice, salt and pepper into a blender. Cover and blend on a low speed until frothy.
2. Cube the butter and put it into a 600 ml (1 pint) measuring jug. Cover loosely with cling film and microwave on HIGH until it melts (1½–2 minutes).
3. With the blender at high speed, very slowly pour in the melted butter, blending until the mixture is very thick and creamy.
4. Pour the mixture back into the measuring jug. Place this in a large bowl containing hand-hot water. (The hot water should be at the same level as the sauce.)
5. Microwave, uncovered, on LOW for 5 minutes or until warm, stirring every 2 minutes. Stir before serving.

Variations

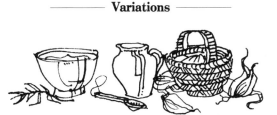

Sauce Béarnaise
Make as for Sauce Hollandaise but begin by putting 60 ml (4 tbsp) of tarragon vinegar with a skinned and chopped shallot, a pinch of cayenne pepper, a sprig of parsley and tarragon into a small heatproof bowl and microwave, uncovered, on HIGH for 3 minutes or until reduced by half. Strain. Proceed as for Sauce Hollandaise.

Sauce Maltaise
Make as for Sauce Hollandaise but use blood-orange juice in place of the lemon juice. Stir in grated or shredded orange rind at the end of cooking if wished.

Sauce Mousseline
Make the basic recipe, cool over ice, then fold in 150 ml (¼ pint) double cream, lightly whipped.

SAFFRON CREAM SAUCE

This vibrant yellow sauce with its mellow flavour suits fish, shellfish, lamb and poultry equally well. Use the hot stock from the main dish you are cooking, if possible. Otherwise use a stock cube and boiling water.

Serves 4

90 ml (6 tbsp) hot stock (lamb, chicken or herb)

1.25 ml (¼ tsp) saffron shreds

60 ml (4 tbsp) double cream

1 egg yolk

salt and freshly ground pepper

1. Measure the stock and saffron shreds into a small heatproof bowl or jug and microwave, uncovered, on HIGH for 1 minute.
2. Leave the dish to stand, stirring from time to time to allow the saffron to infuse the liquid.
3. Add the cream and microwave, uncovered, on HIGH for a further 1½ minutes.
4. Working quickly, add the egg yolk to the sauce, whisking well until the ingredients are blended and slightly thickened. Season and microwave, uncovered, on MEDIUM for 30 seconds. Serve hot.

FRESH TOMATO SAUCE

As with many fruits and vegetables, microwave cooking of tomatoes seems to encourage retention of the full, generous flavour. Sesame oil, herbed vinegar and soft, dark brown sugar each add charm to this refined tomato mixture, which tastes as good as a dip, dressing or sauce. It is most aromatic when served hot or warm.

Serves 4

450 g (1 lb) tomatoes, chopped
1 medium onion, skinned and finely chopped
15 ml (1 tbsp) sesame oil
15 ml (1 tbsp) tarragon vinegar
5 ml (1 level tsp) muscovado sugar
1 fresh bay leaf, crushed
5 ml (1 level tsp) fresh thyme
salt and freshly ground pepper

1. Chop, then purée the tomatoes and onion using a mouli-legumes, food processor, blender or sieve.
2. Put the tomato and onion purée, sesame oil, vinegar, sugar and two herbs into a shallow casserole or heatproof dish, cover with a lid and microwave on HIGH for 3 minutes, stirring, from edges towards the centre, halfway through cooking time.
3. Taste and adjust the seasonings. Remove the herbs if wished, or leave in for a more homely, pungent touch.

Variations

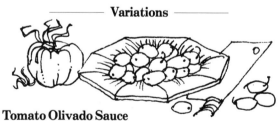

Tomato Olivado Sauce
Make the sauce as above, but stir in 2 tablespoons of tapenade or black olive purée and the same amount of roughly chopped, stoned black olives. This makes a useful dip, spread and dressing.

Pepperami Tomato Sauce
To either of the above sauces add two 40 g (1½ oz) pepperami sausages, sliced thinly, 2 minutes before the end of cooking time. Stir well. This sauce is excellent as a pasta or pizza sauce.

FRUITED FRESH TOMATO SAUCE

This quick but elegant sauce brings a garden sweetness to whatever it accompanies, from pasta and risotto to fish, meat and vegetable dishes. In fact it is quite delicious enough to eat plain, with chunks of good bread, as a dish on its own. In this case it serves two. Alternatively, serve it warm adding crushed and shredded fresh basil, tarragon or thyme leaves, according to your preference.

Serves 2–4

450 g (1 lb) fresh tomatoes
2 shallots, skinned and chopped
15 ml (1 tbsp) virgin olive oil
5 ml (1 level tsp) caster sugar
15 ml (1 tbsp) strawberry, raspberry or other fruit vinegar
salt and freshly ground pepper
fresh herbs of choice (optional)

1. Chop the tomatoes into 1 cm (½ inch) cubes and spread these evenly over the surface of a large, shallow heatproof dish or plate. Add the shallots.
2. Sprinkle with the oil, cover loosely with cling film and microwave on HIGH for 1 minute.
3. Stir from the edges to the centre, and sprinkle with sugar and vinegar. Stir again to mix.
4. Microwave, uncovered, on HIGH for 1 minute more. Add seasoning to taste. Serve hot, rough but stirred, or reduce to a purée using a food processor, blender or sieve.

Above top: Country Cheese and Mustard Dip in radicchio leaves (page 88); Walnut,
Port and Pipe Crem' Dressing (page 86) on potatoes. Overleaf, left to right: Harlequin Capsicums en Papillote (page 68); Pimento
Coulis dip (page 77); Mange-tout in Garlic Dressing (page 69); and Carrot and Orange Julienne (page 74).

Onion Petals with Mustard Butter (page 70); Cauliflower with Rosy Dressing (page 73).

BÉCHAMEL SAUCE

Sauces such as this are bliss to make in a micro-wave oven: lump-free, velvety-textured, creamy-tasting, yet with no risk of scorched saucepans. Since milk-based sauces can and do boil over, it is wise to ensure that the container is large (as specified) to prevent this happening. The variations can be adapted with great versatility to raise good but simple fare to gourmet standard.

Serves 4

300 ml ($\frac{1}{2}$ pint) creamy milk (such as Gold Top)
1 fresh bay leaf, lightly crushed
6 black peppercorns
1 blade mace
1 small onion, peeled
1 clove
1 small carrot, peeled and halved lengthwise
25 g (1 oz) butter
30 ml (2 level tbsp) plain flour
2.5 ml ($\frac{1}{2}$ level tsp) salt

1. Pour the milk into a 900 ml ($1\frac{1}{2}$ pint) heatproof bowl and add the bay leaf, peppercorns, mace, onion stuck with a clove and the carrot. Micro-wave on HIGH for 2 minutes uncovered, then cover and leave to infuse for 10 minutes.
2. Put the butter into a 900 ml ($1\frac{1}{2}$ pint) heatproof measuring jug. Microwave, loosely covered, on HIGH for 30 seconds. Stir in the flour and micro-wave on HIGH for 20 seconds.
3. Strain the infused milk into the butter-flour roux mixture, whisking constantly. Add the salt. Microwave on HIGH for 3 minutes, uncovered, stirring three times during cooking. Whisk again and serve hot.

--- **Variations** ---

Smoky Cheese Sauce
Make Béchamel Sauce as above, but add 75 g (3 oz) grated smoked cheese and 15 ml (1 level tbsp) of Dijon mustard two-thirds of the way through cooking time. Microwave for a final 1 minute, uncovered, stirring twice. Use for vegetable gratin dishes.

Egg and Parsley Sauce
Make Béchamel Sauce as above but add two soft-cooked eggs to the finished sauce. Break the eggs into two buttered 150 ml ($\frac{1}{4}$ pint) ramekins, pricking each egg yolk twice with a wooden cocktail stick. Microwave on MEDIUM, loosely covered by cling film, for 2 minutes. Chop the eggs finely, and stir into the hot sauce with 15 ml (1 level tbsp) chopped fresh parsley. Use with steamed or poached fish dishes, pork and veal.

Caper Sauce
Make Béchamel Sauce as above, then stir in 15 ml (1 level tbsp) drained capers and 10 ml (2 level tsp) white wine vinegar or caper juices. For special occasions, one egg yolk stirred into the cooled caper sauce adds a luxurious effect. Use for herb-poached lamb or mutton, or pan-fried fish.

CREAMY GARLIC PASTA SAUCE

This versatile sauce has great appeal for a variety of dishes besides fresh pasta. Its smooth texture makes it perfect for dipping, spreading and even, if chilled, for stuffing sliced meats such as smoked ham or tongue before they are rolled up to serve as canapés or picnic food. The most important point to note is that unless this cheese mixture is micro-waved on MEDIUM, a grainy mixture will result.

Serves 4

25 g (1 oz) butter
100 ml (4 fl oz) double cream
250 g (9 oz) garlic and herb cream cheese (such as the garlic and herb-type Philadelphia, or Boursin)
5 ml (1 level tsp) prepared herb paste or 15 g ($\frac{1}{2}$ oz) fresh thyme, basil, parsley, marjoram or sage, pounded to a paste
1.25 ml ($\frac{1}{4}$ tsp) freshly ground black pepper

1. Put the butter and cream into a medium heat-proof bowl and microwave on HIGH for 1 minute, uncovered.
2. Pour the butter and cream mixture into a second medium heatproof bowl containing the cream cheese. Beat thoroughly.
3. Add the herb paste and black pepper. Mix thoroughly and microwave on MEDIUM for 3 minutes, uncovered, stirring frequently.

BROWN ONION GRAVY

A quick but satisfactory method for an everyday sauce. Use it when you are serving sliced cold meats, to give a 'just cooked' flavour to the meat. Depending on the additions you make, such as chopped fresh parsley, chopped stuffed olives and so on, it can become even more versatile.

Serves 4

30 ml (2 level tbsp) butter
1 medium onion, skinned and sliced
30 ml (2 level tbsp) flour
250 ml (8 fl oz) homemade stock
50 ml (2 fl oz) red wine
15 ml rich soy sauce

1. Preheat the browning dish on HIGH for 4 minutes.
2. Put the butter in the browning dish with the onion. Microwave on HIGH for 30 seconds, uncovered. Stir in the flour and keep stirring to allow the flour to brown. Microwave, uncovered, on HIGH for 1 minute.
3. Put the stock and wine into a medium heatproof bowl and microwave on HIGH for 2 minutes.
4. Gradually add the stock and wine to the butter and flour. Microwave on HIGH for 2 minutes, uncovered, stirring twice. Add the soy sauce, stir well and serve.

──────── **Variations** ────────

Mushroom Gravy
Make the brown onion gravy as above, adding 125 g (4 oz) sliced mushrooms after stirring in the stock. At the end of the cooking time add 15 ml (1 tbsp) thick cream.

Mushroom Soup
If thinned with half quantities of good stock, this sauce becomes a pleasant soup. Garnish with 15 ml (1 level tbsp) chopped fresh parsley.

WALNUT, PORT AND PIPO CREM' DRESSING

A mellow, pervasive taste of walnut oil dominates this absolutely luxurious dressing. Its colour, a delicate violet-pink, is equally at home on a crisp radicchio salad as over hard-boiled eggs or with small, rosy-pink new potatoes.

Serves 4

100 g (4 oz) Pipo Crem' cheese
30 ml (2 tbsp) walnut oil
75 ml (5 level tbsp) ruby port
25 g (1 oz) shelled walnuts, chopped

1. Combine the Pipo Crem', walnut oil and port.
2. Pour this mixture into a small heatproof serving bowl, cover and microwave on LOW for 1 minute.
3. Stir in the chopped walnuts and serve warm.

See photograph page 81

──────── **COOK'S TIP** ────────
If Pipo Crem' cheese is not available, similar creamy blue cheese such as Gorgonzola or Dolcelatte could be used instead, but do not substitute harsh, lower quality blue cheeses and expect good results.

GRANDMOTHER'S SALAD DRESSING

A basic but useful cooked dressing, especially good for those who find traditional mayonnaise too rich. Sharp and strong, it can be modified by stirring in some thick natural yogurt just before serving. Use it in potato salads, on jacket potatoes and in coleslaw.

Serves 4

1 egg yolk

100 ml (4 fl oz) salad oil

25 ml (1½ tbsp) wine vinegar

10 ml (2 level tsp) flour

45 ml (3 level tbsp) brown sugar

5 ml (1 level tsp) dry mustard

100 ml (4 fl oz) water

2.5 ml (½ level tsp) salt

1 large pinch of cayenne pepper

1 garlic clove, skinned and crushed

1. Put the egg yolk, oil and vinegar into a deep, medium serving dish and then set aside.
2. Combine the flour, sugar and mustard in a medium heatproof bowl, gradually adding the water and mix all the ingredients thoroughly. Microwave on HIGH for 4 minutes, uncovered, stirring several times during cooking.
3. Pour this hot mixture on to the egg mixture, whisking until thickened. Add the salt, cayenne pepper and garlic. Serve chilled.

AUBERGINE DIP CLARA

Whole aubergine cooks beautifully in the microwave oven and breeds new ideas for its use. The first time I tasted aubergine purée was at a friend's table on the island of Aegina in Greece. She told me it was 'Lenten food' suitable for times of fasting, but, with a twinkle in her eye, said it was sinfully rich even so. Next Christmas, in a Trastevere restaurant in Rome, I tasted delicious fresh capelletti pasta filled with a similar purée. I then decided I must re-create a similar dish for myself, so here it is.

Serves 4

450 g (1 lb) aubergines

2 garlic cloves, skinned and crushed

30 ml (2 level tbsp) chopped fresh parsley

5 ml (1 level tsp) fennel seeds, crushed

1.25 ml (¼ tsp) sea salt

50 g (2 oz) walnuts, chopped

60 ml (4 tbsp) strained thick Greek yogurt

Garnish

15 ml (1 level tbsp) chopped parsley or chives

1. Cook the aubergines as for vegetables au naturel (see page 66). Leave to cool, then remove the stem.
2. Cube the aubergine and purée the flesh, using a food processor, blender or mouli-legumes.
3. Combine the remaining ingredients and mix thoroughly with the aubergine purée. Garnish with parsley or chives.

— COOK'S TIP —
Briefly heated, the dip can serve as a spread for hors-d'oeuvres or cocktail snacks; cold, it can be used to fill pasta or vol-au-vent cases, or to spread on open sandwiches.

COUNTRY CHEESE AND MUSTARD DIP

Powerful flavours lurk in this hot dip, which is served like a fondue with a selection of foods for dipping. It is substantial enough to serve two as a complete lunch, or supper if digestion permits, washed down with good, cold cider.

Serves 2–4

225 g (8 oz) farmhouse cheddar cheese
100 g (4 oz) Cotswold cheese
15 ml (1 level tbsp) fécule (potato starch) or cornflour
1 small onion
200 ml (⅓ pint) dry cider
15 ml (1 tbsp) Worcestershire sauce
15 ml (1 level tbsp) tarragon mustard or herb mustard
2 spring onions, finely sliced
30 ml (2 tbsp) dry gin

1. Coarsely grate the cheeses and toss together with the fécule in a bowl. Skin and coarsely grate the onion and add to the mixture.
2. Pour the cider into a deep 600 ml (1 pint) casserole. Microwave on HIGH, uncovered, for 1½–2 minutes or until bubbles start to appear. Do not boil.
3. Stir in half the prepared mixture, blending well. Microwave, uncovered, on HIGH for 2 minutes or until the cheese is almost melted.
4. Stir in the remaining mixture, adding the Worcestershire sauce, mustard and onions.

5. Microwave on HIGH, uncovered, for 2–3 minutes or until the cheese is almost melted. Whisk until smooth, adding the gin gradually.

See photograph page 81

───── **SERVING TIP** ─────
Serve hot with cheese straws, crisp cheese crackers or granary bread chunks and, for dipping, slices of sharp-flavoured eating apples such as Cox's Orange Pippins.

CREAMY LOVAGE AND ORANGE DIP

The aromatic effect of herbs is often accentuated by microwave cooking, and can be well exploited. Wonderful served with or after iced soup (or vegetable soup of any kind), this refreshing creation has a taste of the country about it. Do it the honour of serving it with really good bread. (Flat leaf parsley may be used instead of lovage, but the flavour will not have that extra special quality.)

Serves 4–6

25 g (1 oz) butter
1 small onion, skinned and finely chopped
175 g (6 oz) cream cheese
30 ml (2 level tbsp) chopped fresh parsley
15 ml (1 level tbsp) chopped fresh lovage
10 ml (2 level tsp) finely grated orange rind
30 ml (2 tbsp) fresh orange juice
salt and freshly ground pepper

1. Put the butter and onion into a 600 ml (1 pint) heatproof serving bowl. Loosely cover with cling film and microwave on HIGH for 1 minute, stirring halfway through the cooking time.
2. Add the cream cheese and chopped herbs. Loosely cover with cling film and microwave on MEDIUM for 2 minutes.
3. Add the orange rind and juice and microwave

on MEDIUM for a further minute, covered as before.

4. Season to taste and serve hot or cold with heated French bread, wholewheat bread sticks or dark rye bread chunks.

CARAMEL AND LIME GLAZE

This glaze can be poured over plainly-cooked turkey, duck, guinea-fowl, pheasant, rabbit, hare joints, or whole baked fish when they have finished cooking, and can then be heated briefly. Alternatively, it can be used as the cooking liquid (with a knob of butter added) for quickly-cooked pork chops and gammon steaks, lean pork chipolatas, and lamb chops or cutlets. It can also give a very elegant look to any dish if the plate is first 'mirrored' with the glaze and the cooked food, with a suitable garnish, is then placed upon it.

'Mirroring' is achieved by pouring some sauce into the centre of a serving plate, which is then tilted and rotated so that the liquid evenly covers the surface.

Serves 4–6

2 fresh limes
225 g (8 oz) granulated sugar
150 ml (¼ pint) water
15 ml (1 level tbsp) gin or vodka

1. Shred the rind from the two limes using a zester, or pare the rind and then slice it into thread-like strips. Squeeze the juice from one lime. Discard the pith from the other lime and then slice the flesh thinly. Quarter the slices and reserve the rind, juice and lime flesh.
2. Spread just 200 g (7 oz) of the sugar evenly over the surface of a 25 cm (10 inch) browning dish. Microwave, uncovered, on HIGH for 4 minutes, turning the dish once halfway through cooking time. (Even so, sugar caramelises more in some areas than others.) Do not stir.
3. Standing well back to avoid steam burns, pour the water slowly over the caramel. Add the remaining 25 g (1 oz) sugar and microwave on HIGH for a further 4 minutes, uncovered, stirring once.

4. Add the liquor, reserved lime rind, juice and flesh.

———— **Variation** ————

Masking Glaze
For a thicker coating or masking glaze (such as for cold poultry, meat or game) add 2 teaspoons of arrowroot, stirred into 2 tablespoons of cold water. Microwave on HIGH for 1½–2 minutes, stirring every 30 seconds. Cool before pouring over cold poultry, meat or game, and garnish with herbs.

HONEY, SAGE AND GARLIC GLAZE

This glaze can be used with cuts of chicken, pork, bacon and lamb. First marinade and then cook them in it briefly to form a glaze and sauce simultaneously. (Do not, however, use it for long-cooked dishes.) It can also be used to 'dress' cold cooked game or poultry.

Serves 4

120 ml (8 level tbsp) honey
100 ml (4 fl oz) water
2 garlic cloves, skinned and crushed
15 ml (1 tbsp) rich soy sauce
15 ml (1 level tbsp) French mustard
3–4 sprigs of sage
15 ml (1 level tbsp) arrowroot
10 ml (2 tsp) lemon juice

1. Put the honey, water, garlic, soy sauce, mustard and sage sprigs into a bowl and mix well. Microwave, uncovered, on HIGH for 3 minutes.
2. Blend the arrowroot with 30 ml (2 tbsp) cold water and stir into the mixture. Microwave on HIGH for 1 minute, stirring every 20 seconds.
3. Allow to cool, then add the lemon juice.

S·W·E·E·T A·N·D S·A·V·O·U·R·Y P·R·E·S·E·R·V·E·S

PICKLED MUSHROOMS KOTA BHARU

In spite of a somewhat eclectic choice of ingredients, this is a special pickle. Mediterranean olive oil, Mexican honey and English button mushrooms all feature. But finally and most important, sesame oil, hot chilli and lemon grass from Malaysia made me decide on the Malaysian name. Fresh lemon grass, available from Asian supermarkets, is formed rather like the bulb of a spring onion. It must be cut lengthwise at right angles to give long, slender, aromatic shreds. The fresh red chilli curls up into flower shaped petals (its stem intact).

Makes 900 g (2 lb)

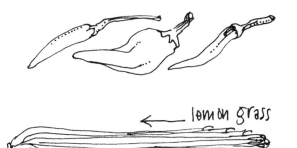

lemon grass

cut lengthwise......

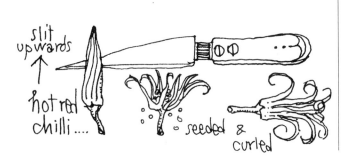

slit upwards

hot red chilli....

seeded & curled

30 ml (2 tbsp) fruity olive oil
15 ml (1 tbsp) sesame oil
450 g (1 lb) whole button mushrooms
2 garlic cloves, skinned and chopped
30 ml (2 tbsp) flower-scented honey
50 ml (2 fl oz) white or rose wine
75 ml (5 level tbsp) red wine vinegar
1 hot red chilli, slit several times lengthwise and seeded
15 g (½ oz) bulb and stem of lemon grass, cut lengthwise into 4 pieces

To seal

30 ml (2 tbsp) fruity olive oil

1. Preheat a 25 cm (10 inch) browning dish on HIGH for 8 minutes, or according to the manufacturer's instructions. Add the olive and sesame oils, then the mushrooms and garlic. Shake the dish to toss the mushrooms in the oil. Microwave, uncovered, on HIGH for 4 minutes, stirring twice, until the mushrooms are tender and have shrunk in size.

2. Add the remaining ingredients (except the olive oil to seal) and microwave, uncovered, for a further 4 minutes on HIGH until boiling.

3. Pour into hot sterilized jars (see page 93) with a tightly fitting lid. When cold, pour the extra 30 ml (2 tbsp) olive oil gently over the surface of the mushrooms to act as a seal, and replace the lid securely.

--- COOK'S TIP ---

Serve these mushrooms, with the liquid for dressing, on their own as tiny hors d'oeuvres, sliced into salads, as part of an open sandwich or with smoked fish or cured hams. They are a delight to have in your store cupboard.

GREEN MANGO CHUTNEY ALPHONSO

This delicious chutney is a truly mouth-watering condiment. It is my own simplification of the type of Indian dish usually cooked for hours and then left in the sun to 'ripen' for some weeks. Such impatient persons as myself wish to achieve the authentic effect without weeks of care and this microwave version provides the answer.

Note that immature mangoes are used, and not the large ripe variety. The seed or stone of these golfball-sized fruit is white and pliable, and is discarded before cooking. Befriend your local Asian greengrocer or specialist supplier: baby green mangoes are to be found among their stock.

Leave the skinned, seeded mangoes in halves, without further chopping. It is pleasant to come across chunky pieces of the fruit. (The name Alphonso is that of a variety of mango.)

Makes 900 g (2 lb)

350 g (12 oz) small, unripe green mangoes
300 ml (½ pint) garlic flavoured wine vinegar
100 g (4 oz) light, soft brown sugar
10 ml (2 tsp) salt
50 g (2 oz) black mustard seeds
100 g (4 oz) fresh root ginger, food processed or coarsely grated
50 g (2 oz) garlic cloves, skinned and finely chopped
5 ml (1 level tsp) fenugreek
7.5–10 ml (1½–2 level tsp) cayenne pepper
5 ml (1 level tsp) turmeric
100 g (4 oz) seeded raisins

1. Halve the mangoes lengthwise, remove and discard the soft white stone and scoop or turn out the flesh, discarding the skin. Put into a medium heatproof bowl with 50 ml (2 fl oz) of the vinegar. Cover ⅞ of the bowl with cling film and microwave on HIGH for 5 minutes, stirring halfway through cooking time. The fruit should look pulpy.
2. In a second medium heatproof bowl, put the remainder of the vinegar, all the sugar and the salt. Stir, then microwave on HIGH, uncovered, for 4 minutes or until the mixture boils. Pour the hot contents of the second bowl into the mango-vinegar mixture and blend in the remaining ingredients.

3. Microwave on HIGH, uncovered, for 15 minutes, stirring every 5 minutes from the outside to the centre. The chutney should be well reduced and syrupy in consistency.
4. Pour, while still hot, into hot sterilized jars (see page 93), cover with waxed discs, cellophane and rubber bands. Alternatively, use jars with ground glass stoppers. This pickle can be used immediately or stored for long term use.

ANANAS ACETO DOLCE

Fresh pineapple pickled in this way is absolutely delicious for use throughout the year. It complements mild, soft, creamy cheeses, is good with cured beef, smoked or cured ham and can enliven a coleslaw or potato salad if used with discretion.

Makes 450 g (1 lb)

1 large ripe pineapple, 1.6 kg (3½ lb)
about 50 cloves
225 ml (8 fl oz) white wine vinegar
10 ml (2 level tsp) mustard seeds
1.25 ml (¼ tsp) chilli powder
100 g (4 oz) light soft brown sugar
50 g (2 oz) honey

1. Slice the whole pineapple crosswise into rings 2 cm (¾ inch) thick. Slice off and discard the tough outer skin, making six cuts to give a hexagonal shape. Cut the flesh into 6 even-sized triangles and stud each triangle with one clove. The final yield should be about 700 g (1½ lb).
2. Stir the remaining ingredients together and pour over the pineapple pieces. Microwave, uncovered, on HIGH for 20 minutes or until the syrup has reduced and the pineapple is very tender.
3. Leave to stand for 5 minutes before transferring to a hot sterilized jar (see page 93). Cover, seal and label. Eat fresh or use as a preserve.

CRUNCHY COLESLAW PICKLE

This fresh, salady pickle can be used on the same day it is made, or kept for up to a month (in a cool, dark place) for use with chicken, turkey, ham and other cold meats. The sweet-sour liquid can also be added to mayonnaise or soured cream, or used as a marinade.

Makes 1.4 kg (3 lb)

450 g (1 lb) celery sticks, thinly sliced

450 g (1 lb) onions, skinned and thinly sliced

225 g (8 oz) cauliflower in tiny florets

2 ripe comice pears, peeled, cored and cubed

450 g (1 lb) granulated sugar

30 ml (2 level tbsp) salt

10 ml (2 level tsp) pale mustard seeds

5 ml (1 level tsp) crushed mace blades

10 ml (2 level tsp) turmeric

5 ml (1 level tsp) cumin seeds, lightly crushed

450 ml (15 fl oz) white wine or dry vermouth

300 ml ($\frac{1}{2}$ pint) white vinegar

1. Put the prepared sliced celery, onions, cauliflower and pears into a large bowl and cover with boiling water. Leave to stand for 10 minutes, drain well in a colander then pat dry between 2 layers of absorbent kitchen paper.
2. Spoon the blanched and dried vegetables into six 225 g (8 oz) sterilized pots or jars (see page 93) and keep aside while preparing the syrup.
3. Put the remaining ingredients in a deep, heat-proof bowl. Stir well and cover $\frac{7}{8}$ of the top with cling film. Microwave on HIGH for 7 minutes, stirring twice. Uncover the bowl and microwave, uncovered, on HIGH for a further 7 minutes.
4. Pour the boiling syrup into the sterilized pots or jars until the vegetables are covered. Cover each pot or jar with a waxed disc, seal with cellophane and secure with a rubber band.

FRESH CORIANDER AND GINGER CHUTNEY

An Indian-influenced recipe creates this 'fresh' or short storage-life chutney. The onions are mellowed first, by cooking, but the herbs keep their pungency. Stir the chutney into yogurt, mayonnaise or rice to give them fragrance and serve with curried meat, fish, poultry, game or vegetables.

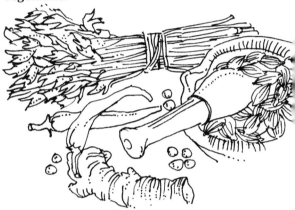

Makes 1.1 kg (2$\frac{1}{2}$ lb)

30 ml (2 tbsp) virgin olive oil

900 g (2 lb) Spanish onions, skinned and chopped

3 garlic cloves, skinned and chopped

25 g (1 oz) fresh ginger root, coarsely grated

1 fresh green chilli, seeded and chopped

225 g (8 oz) fresh coriander leaves and stems, roughly chopped

30 ml (2 tbsp) freshly squeezed lemon juice

15 ml (1 level tbsp) salt

30 ml (2 level tbsp) caster sugar

1. Pour the olive oil into a shallow heatproof dish and microwave on HIGH for 1 minute. Add the onions, garlic and ginger. Microwave, covered with cling film or a lid, on HIGH for 6 minutes, stirring halfway through cooking time.
2. Put the chopped chilli and coriander into a food processor or blender. Spoon in the hot mixture and add the lemon juice, salt and sugar. Process until blended (chopped but not puréed) for about 30 seconds, no longer.
3. Spoon into hot sterilized jars (see page 93). Cover, seal and label and store in the refrigerator or in a cool, dark place. Use within a few weeks.

TIPSY PEACH AND CARDAMOM CONSERVE

It gladdens the heart to invent a recipe which needs few but very select ingredients and which yields, without undue effort, such poetical results. This exquisite conserve seems a fitting tribute to the peaches of the proud T'ang emperors and to the modest French soldier, Girardot, who through his friend the royal gardener, offered his perfect peaches anonymously to King Louis XIV.

Makes 550 g (1¼ lb)

800 g (1¾ lb) fresh, white fleshed peaches

15 green cardamom seed pods

150 ml (¼ pint) rosé or white wine

30 ml (2 tbsp) freshly squeezed orange juice

450 g (1 lb) granulated sugar

1. Slice the unpeeled flesh from the peaches to remove the stones, giving 6–8 pieces of flesh from each fruit. Place the flesh in a medium heatproof bowl.
2. Using a small hammer or rolling pin, crack the peach stones to extract the white kernels and break the cardamom pods to remove the small black seeds. Add the kernels and cardamom seeds to the bowl with the rosé wine and orange juice. Microwave, uncovered, on HIGH for 6–7 minutes. Test this juice for its pectin content (see below).
3. Add the sugar and microwave, uncovered, on HIGH for 14–16 minutes, stirring gently from time to time. The conserve will become golden pink and syrupy. A teaspoonful placed on a chilled saucer should form a skin after 1 minute, indicating a good degree of setting.
4. Leave the conserve to stand for 3–5 minutes then stir gently to distribute the fruit evenly throughout. Pour, while still quite hot, into hot sterilized jars (see Cook's tip). Cover with a waxed disc and seal with cellophane secured with a rubber band. Label.

To test for pectin
Place 5 ml (1 tsp) of the juice to be tested in a cup or glass. Leave until cold, then add 15 ml (1 tbsp) of methylated spirits. Shake gently and leave to stand for 1 minute. One or two jelly-like clots indicate the presence of sufficient pectin to set the jam. If there are only many small, soft clots then commercial pectin must be added in the manufacturer's recommended quantities to ensure successful results.

HEDONISTS' SCARLET STRAWBERRY JAM

Microwave ovens are most suitable for making small amounts of jams and preserves. Turn this to advantage by making one delectable pot at a time for the next day's breakfast. It was Lewis Carroll who in Through the Looking Glass *said 'jam tomorrow, jam yesterday – but never jam today'. This recipe could defy his rule because the jam is delicious eaten very fresh and still warm. It is true strawberry coloured, has mouthwatering syrupy juices and is superb spooned over fromage frais or thick natural yogurt, ice cream, hot scones or toast. A little Cointreau may be poured over the top of each jar before sealing.*

450 g (1 lb) fresh strawberries, washed and hulled

25 ml (1½ tbsp) lemon juice

350 g (12 oz) granulated sugar

15 ml (1 tbsp) Cointreau or Grand Marnier (optional)

1. Put the strawberries, slightly crushed, and lemon juice into a deep heatproof bowl, cover with cling film and microwave on HIGH for 5 minutes.
2. Stir in the sugar and microwave on HIGH for a further 14 minutes.
3. Allow to cool and pour into sterilized jars (see below). If wished, spoon the Cointreau or Grand Marnier carefully over the top.
4. Cover, seal and label.

—— COOK'S TIP ——
To sterilize jars in the microwave oven: pour in 60 ml (4 tbsp) water and microwave on HIGH for 1½ minutes or until boiling. Using oven gloves, pour out the water and invert the jar on to clean absorbent kitchen paper or a sterile oven rack and the hot jar is ready for use.

CHERRY PRESERVE FORT ENDA

Preserve two treasured pots or jars of those cherries (never many) left over during the cherry season. Use sparingly: these are luscious. They can be lifted to the mouth, stems and all and their syrup sampled as a homely type of ratafia, in tiny chilled glasses. The syrup could otherwise be used as the basis of a vodka or gin cocktail, or even as a cherry version of the famous Kir, mixed with chilled white burgundy.

The war hero Giuseppe Galliano literally 'held the fort' for 44 days before surrendering, and try to sample the cherries within this time-span to enjoy them at their best.

Makes two 175 g (6 oz) pots or jars

225 g (8 oz) whole fresh cherries with stems
90 ml (6 tbsp) unsweetened white grape juice
100 g (4 oz) caster sugar
60 ml (4 tbsp) Galliano (or, if unavailable, Yellow Chartreuse)

1. Wash the cherries and dry them by rolling carefully in absorbent kitchen paper. Do not remove the stems.
2. Using a fine needle, prick each cherry to the stone in 6 or 8 places. Sterilize two 175 g (6 oz) pots or glass jars (see page 93) and fill them with the cherries.
3. Put the grape juice and sugar in a medium heatproof bowl and microwave, uncovered, on HIGH for 6 minutes, stirring twice.
4. Carefully pour the hot syrup over the cherries. Space the 2 pots evenly in the oven and micro-wave, uncovered, on HIGH for 2 minutes, rearranging their positions halfway through cooking time.
5. Pour 1 tablespoon of the chosen liqueur into each pot. Cover each with a waxed disc, seal with cellophane and secure with a rubber band. Otherwise use a ground glass stopper or non-metal lid. Store in a cool, dark place.

See photograph page 103

GUAVA AND CUSTARD-APPLE HONEY

Custard-apples are heart-shaped fruits with a strange, green skin like dense armour plate. Inside is the most delectable, silken, cream-coloured flesh which tastes not unlike sweetened condensed milk. It is a revelation. Guavas (although commonly available in canned form) are, when bought fresh, strange-scented fruits, gently egg-shaped and filled with succulent flesh. I first tasted both custard apples and guavas in Singapore. They can now be found here on ethnic market stalls and in specialist food stores.

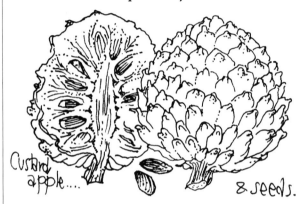

Custard apple....   & seeds.

Makes 450 g (1 lb)

700 g (1½ lb) fresh custard apples (sweetsops)
225–275 g (8–10 oz) fresh guavas
225 g (8 oz) granulated sugar
15 ml (1 tbsp) freshly squeezed lemon juice

1. Halve the custard apples lengthwise. Using a spoon, scoop out the flesh from each half so that it remains in one piece. Cut it crosswise into slices so as to remove all the black seeds. Weigh the flesh: there should be about 450 g (1 lb).
2. Halve the guavas crosswise. Using a spoon, scoop out the flesh and chop roughly.
3. Put the custard apple and guava flesh into a medium heatproof bowl, add 45 ml (3 tbsp) water, cover with cling film and microwave on HIGH for 7 minutes, stirring once halfway through cooking time.
4. Rub the fruit through a fine sieve to obtain a smooth white purée. Return the purée to the bowl, add the sugar and lemon juice and stir to blend.
5. Cover $\frac{7}{8}$ of the bowl with cling film and micro-

wave on HIGH for 10 minutes, stirring once half-way through. The texture should be thick but creamy.

6. While still hot, pour into hot sterilized jars (see page 93), cover with waxed discs, cellophane and rubber bands. Store in a cool, dark place to prevent any deterioration of the unique flavours.

──────── **SERVING TIP** ────────

This spread retains a pearly white colour. Use it sparingly on freshly made tea-bread, with brioches or with hot croissants for breakfast. Alternatively, use it diluted with some white wine as a sauce/dressing for other fruits, for game or for marinated raw fish salads.

SATSUMA AND LEMON CURD

This refreshing breakfast spread is also good enough to use as a filling for a sweet pastry flan with meringue, or for folding into thick natural yogurt (with nuts added) as a simple dessert. Satsuma adds an elegant scentedness to the curd.

Makes 450 g (1 lb)

juice and grated rind of 3 satsumas
juice and grated rind of 1 lemon
100 g (4 oz) butter, cut into pieces
250 g (9 oz) caster sugar
3 eggs, at room temperature
1 egg yolk, at room temperature

1. Put the fruit rinds, juices and butter into a large heatproof bowl. Microwave, uncovered, on HIGH for 3 minutes. Add the sugar and microwave, uncovered, on HIGH for a further 2 minutes. Stir well.

2. Beat together the eggs and egg yolk and blend quickly but thoroughly into the hot satsuma and lemon mixture. Microwave, uncovered, on LOW (30%) for 12 minutes, stirring from edge to centre every 3 minutes, or until the mixture is creamy and thick.

3. Pour into hot sterilized jars (see page 93). Cover, seal and label.

APPLE AND ROSE GERANIUM JELLY

This fruit jelly, made aromatic by the crushed leaves of scented geranium, has a tender, fragile set and an old-fashioned pale tint. Float a blanched, well-dried fresh rose geranium leaf in each jar before sealing, for an extra pretty effect.

I have found that a plastic sieve, used in place of the traditional jelly bag for extracting the juice, is convenient and works well. Rather than discard the apple and geranium pulp, it can be rubbed through the same sieve to give a purée from which a fruit butter can be made by a second cooking process. In less than 3 hours you will have made jelly. In another 30 minutes you will also have an exotic-tasting fruit spread. Microwave magic!

Makes 350–450 g (12 oz–1 lb)

900 g (2 lb) tart-flavoured eating apples (such as Granny Smith)
6–8 fresh rose (or other) scented geranium leaves
300 ml ($\frac{1}{2}$ pint) water
250 g (9 oz) granulated sugar

1. Quarter the apples and place in a medium heat-proof bowl with the geranium leaves and the water. Cover with cling film and microwave on HIGH for 10 minutes, stirring once halfway through the cooking time. Purée the cooked apples and their liquid in a blender or food processor and carefully allow to drip, undisturbed, through a fine sieve for $1\frac{1}{2}$ hours. Reserve the fruit pulp to make apple and rum butter (page 96).

2. Make up the quantity of strained apple juice, about 100 ml (4 fl oz), to 300 ml ($\frac{1}{2}$ pint) with water. Add the sugar, place in a medium heat-proof bowl and microwave, uncovered, on HIGH for 10–12 minutes, stirring occasionally. A teaspoonful dropped on a cold saucer should form a skin on the surface after 1 minute to indicate a successful setting quality.

3. Pour into one or more hot sterilized jars (see page 93). Cover each with a waxed disc and seal with cellophane and a rubber band. Label.

QUINCE AND APPLE JELLY

Traditional rosy-hued jelly is here made from traditional ingredients, but the use of purchased apple juice helps to boost its colour. Microwave cooking seems to retain all the original taste of fruits such as these. Use the jelly with game, on hot scones and for glazes.

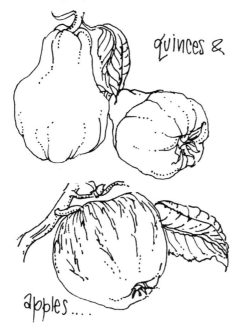

quinces &

apples....

Makes 450 g (1 lb)

| 900 g (2 lb) tart eating apples, quartered |
| 450 g (1 lb) quinces, thinly sliced |
| 600 ml (1 pint) water |
| juice of 1 lemon |
| 100 ml (4 fl oz) unsweetened apple juice |
| 250 g (9 oz) granulated sugar |

1. Put the apples, quinces and water into a large heatproof bowl. Cover with cling film and microwave on HIGH for 20–22 minutes, stirring frequently. Process using a food processor or blender, then allow the juices to drip through a fine nylon sieve for 1½ hours. Reserve the pulp to make Quince and Apple Butter if wished. (See below.)
2. Make up the quantity of strained juices, about 175 ml (6 fl oz), to 300 ml (½ pint) with unsweetened apple juice. Add the lemon juice and place in a large heatproof bowl with the sugar.

Stir well and microwave, uncovered, on HIGH for 12–14 minutes or until a good result is achieved with the 'setting' pectin test (see page 93).
3. Pour into hot sterilized jars (see page 93) and cover each with a waxed disc. Seal with cellophane, secure with a rubber band and label.

───── COOK'S TIP ─────
To make Quince and Apple Butter, see Apple and Rum Butter, but allow 1 part of sugar to each 2 parts of strained, weighed fruit purée. Cook until setting consistency is obtained, then pour into hot sterilized jars. Cover, seal and label.

APPLE AND RUM BUTTER

This recipe uses the apple pulp (puréed until smooth using a nylon sieve) left over from the Apple and Rose Geranium Jelly (page 95). It has a buttery-firm spreading texture and the rum provides a faint but definite flavour boost.

Makes 350 g (12 oz)

| 450 ml (15 fl oz) cooked apple and geranium pulp |
| 175 g (6 oz) granulated sugar |
| 15 ml (1 tbsp) dark rum |

1. Rub the apple and geranium pulp through a nylon sieve to give a smooth purée. Combine this purée with the sugar in a medium heatproof bowl. Stir well and microwave, uncovered, on HIGH for 16–18 minutes until a thickened buttery mixture is reached.
2. Stir in the rum and pour, while still hot, into hot sterilized jars (see page 93). Cover each with a waxed disc. Seal with cellophane and secure with a rubber band. Label.

D·E·S·S·E·R·T·S, C·A·K·E·S AND C·U·S·T·A·R·D·S

AMARETTI PEARS ROSÉ

One day I intend to visit Saronno, home of the enchanting little paper-wrapped macaroon biscuits. Until that time I can content myself with using them in this elegant baked pear recipe.

Serves 4

4 firm William pears, stems intact
8 Amaretti de Saronno biscuits
2 drops almond essence
30 ml (2 tbsp) liquid honey
150 ml ($\frac{1}{4}$ pint) rosé wine
5 ml (1 level tsp) arrowroot

1. Peel the pears carefully and core them, reserving the top section containing the stem.
2. Roughly crush the Amaretti de Saronno biscuits and use them to fill the core cavities almost to the top. Replace the top stem sections and stand the pears upright in a shallow heatproof casserole.
3. Stir the almond essence into the honey and spoon or trickle the honey over the pears to coat them. Pour all but 2 tablespoons of wine into the dish.
4. Microwave, uncovered, on HIGH for 3–4 minutes or until just tender. Transfer the pears to serving dishes. Mix the arrowroot with the reserved wine and pour into the dish. Microwave on HIGH for 20 seconds, stirring once with a wooden spoon halfway through cooking time.
5. Spoon the hot sauce-glaze over the pears and serve hot after allowing them to stand for at least 2 minutes.

MEDITERRANEAN NECTARINES

When sun-ripened perfect nectarines are available, try stoning, stuffing and then baking them whole in a microwave oven. Prepared this way they remain blushing pink, taste delicious and are magically quick! The surprise is the stuffing, melted to a sauce, which flows out when the fruit is broken into with a spoon. Prepare them in advance to cook later and eat on the spot. They should always be served straight away as the skins, alas, discolour on standing.

Serves 4

4 fresh nectarines, ripe but undamaged
30 ml (2 level tbsp) chopped pistachio nuts
15 ml (1 level tbsp) muscovado sugar

1. To stone the nectarines, hold them firmly in the hand and, using your thumb, press from the stalk end to push the stone out through the other side. Carefully reshape the fruits and arrange them round the edge of a heatproof plate with the clean thumb hole facing upwards.
2. Mix together the pistachio nuts and muscovado sugar and use them to fill each nectarine cavity. Microwave, uncovered, for $4\frac{1}{2}$ minutes on MEDIUM, giving the plate a half turn halfway through cooking. Allow to stand for just 1 minute before serving.

SERVING TIP

Try serving with whipped cream flavoured with a little golden rum. A soft, scented Sauternes or an eau-de-vie such as Reine-Claude, Fraise or Framboise would be the charming foil for such a lovely dessert.

WRAPPED FIGS WITH PRALINE BUTTER

Plump Italian figs with Danish unsalted butter and praline (containing American pecans) for the stuffing — this recipe is international indeed! Add the fillip of French, Greek or Turkish aniseed-flavoured spirit for the final touch. Wrap in a wisp of paper and behold — a new delectable creation for the microwave oven, tempting the eyes as well as the tongue.

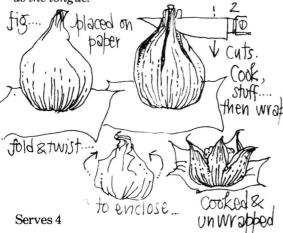

Serves 4

25 g (1 oz) unsalted butter
15 ml (1 level tbsp) powdered praline
10 ml (2 tsp) Ricard, Ouzo or Raki
4 firm ripe fresh figs

1. Blend together the butter, praline and Ricard (or other aniseed flavoured spirit of your choice).
2. Place four pieces of greaseproof paper, each 15 cm (6 inch) square, on the floor of the microwave oven, evenly spaced from the centre. Take the figs and make 2 crosswise cuts part way down from top to base of each fig so that they open like flowers. Place one of the figs on each square of paper. Microwave, uncovered, on HIGH for 1 minute.
3. Divide the flavoured butter between the figs, pushing a spoonful into the centre of each. Bring up the corners of the paper squares and lightly twist to form little parcels. Microwave for a further 45 seconds on HIGH.
4. Serve, still wrapped, so the diners may unwrap their own delicious fig parcels. Eat with chilled, strained, natural thick yogurt, crème fraîche or fromage blanc.

See photograph page 102

FLAMBÉED BANANAS WITH LIME

This classic dessert is so good and effortless that you'll wonder why you don't make it more often. The freshness of both orange liqueur and lime flesh (pith removed) is delectable.

Serves 4

50 g (2 oz) unsalted butter
4 bananas, each diagonally sliced into 4
25 g (1 oz) muscovado sugar
shredded rind of 1 lime
squeezed juice of ½ lime
chopped flesh of ½ lime
30 ml (2 tbsp) Cointreau or Curaçao

1. Put the butter in a shallow, heatproof serving dish. Microwave, uncovered, on HIGH for 1½ minutes to melt and heat the butter.
2. Add the bananas in one layer, shaking the dish to roll and coat them with butter. Microwave, uncovered, on HIGH for 2 minutes, shaking briskly halfway through the cooking time.
3. Sprinkle over the sugar, shredded rind, the lime juice and lime flesh. Microwave, uncovered, on HIGH for a further minute.
4. Measure the Cointreau into a small heatproof bowl or cup and microwave, uncovered, on HIGH for 20 seconds or until warm. Remove from the microwave oven.
5. Ignite the Cointreau with a taper, holding well away from the face, and pour the flaming contents over the bananas. Serve while still 'flamboyant'.

――――― **SERVING TIP** ―――――
This dessert is excellent served with strained natural yogurt or thick cream.

RASPBERRY AND ROSE CHARLOTTE

I discovered the affinity raspberry has for rose when, as a newly-wed, I used red rose petals from our first New Zealand garden to scatter over homemade raspberry ice cream. In this recipe, rosewater modifies both the glaze for the biscuits and the gently set fruit filling. Since commercially made Boudoir biscuits can vary in size, I have recommended using 16–20. Serve the dessert on the day it is made or the biscuits lose their charm.

Serves 6–8

100 g (4 oz) raspberry seedless jelly
30 ml (2 tbsp) freshly squeezed lemon juice
few drops rosewater or orange juice
16–20 Boudoir (or sponge finger) biscuits
15 ml (1 level tbsp) gelatine
450 g (1 lb) raspberries
2 egg yolks
5 ml (1 tsp) rosewater
225 g (8 oz) double cream, lightly whipped

Decoration

150 ml (¼ pint) whipping cream
30 ml (2 level tbsp) caster sugar

1. Line the sides of a 15 cm (6 inch) round spring-form or loose-bottom cake or charlotte tin with foil. Lightly oil the base and sides.
2. Put the raspberry jelly and lemon juice into a shallow heatproof bowl. Microwave, uncovered, on HIGH for 3 minutes, stirring from time to time. Stir in the rosewater or orange juice.
3. Carefully dip each biscuit, sugar side down, in the hot syrup and then use them to line the sides of the tin. Position them carefully so that they support each other. Use the remaining syrup to brush over the inner surface of the biscuits.
4. Put 45 ml (3 tbsp) cold water in a small heat-proof bowl and sprinkle the gelatine over it. Allow it to become firm. Microwave on HIGH for 1

minute, or until the gelatine is dissolved, stirring well.
5. Purée the raspberries in a food processor or blender. Whisk in the egg yolks one at a time, add 5 ml (1 tbsp) rosewater and the melted gelatine, pouring in a steady stream. When nearly set, fold this into the lightly whipped double cream. Pour into the centre of the prepared cake tin and refrigerate for 2–3 hours, or until set.
6. Just before serving, remove the charlotte from the tin and carefully peel away the foil, pulling downwards. Lightly whip and sweeten the whipping cream with the caster sugar, then spoon or pipe it into the centre of the pudding.
7. Serve the charlotte whole and cut, like a cake, into wedges.

HOT BRAMBLE FOOL

Since the word 'fool' probably derives from the French verb fouler, *meaning to crush, I feel I can use it for this somewhat unorthodox recipe. The microwave oven helps to retain the original colour of the berries, so that a brilliant colour results. This sweet, frothy dessert is made to be eaten immediately, while still warm.*

Serves 4

2 egg whites, at room temperature
100 g (4 oz) icing sugar
225 g (8 oz) blackberries
30 ml (2 tbsp) gin

1. Whisk the egg whites until stiff peaks have formed. Gradually whisk in just 75 g (3 oz) of the icing sugar.
2. Put the blackberries into a medium heatproof bowl with the remaining 25 g (1 oz) of icing sugar. Microwave, uncovered, on HIGH for 2 minutes. Stir in the gin and crush the berries gently but thoroughly.
3. Gently fold the blackberries into the meringue mixture and serve immediately, while still warm and frothy, in stemmed glasses.

GREENGAGE AND AMARETTO UPSIDE-DOWN PUDDING

To me, greengages symbolise the profligate pleasures of summer – their dappled green sweetness a brief but specific gift. This delightful pudding would ideally be served warm with lightly whipped cream or that deliciously rich tasting strained Greek yogurt.

Serves 6–8

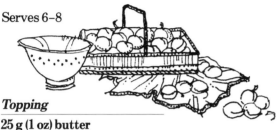

Topping

25 g (1 oz) butter

30 ml (2 tbsp) golden syrup

275 g (10 oz) greengages, halved and stoned

25 g (1 oz) blanched almonds

Pudding

175 g (6 oz) butter

175 g (6 oz) soft golden brown sugar

1.25 ml ($\frac{1}{4}$ tsp) almond essence

3 eggs

175 g (6 oz) plain flour

30 ml (2 level tbsp) baking powder

Decoration

25 g (1 oz) pistachio nuts, coarsely chopped

15–30 ml (1–2 tbsp) Amaretto or other almond-flavoured liqueur

1. Lightly grease a 23 cm (9 inch) microwave ring mould.
2. Place the butter and golden syrup in the base of the mould and microwave on HIGH for 20 seconds.
3. Arrange the greengages in the dish, cut side down, with one almond in the centre of each.
4. To make the pudding mixture, cream the butter and sugar together until light and fluffy. Add the almond essence. Add the eggs, one at a time, beating well. Sieve together the flour and baking powder and fold these ingredients into the pudding mixture.
5. Spoon the mixture carefully over the greengages and smooth over the top.
6. Cover lightly with baking parchment and microwave on HIGH for 12 minutes. Rotate, one half turn, halfway through cooking time.
7. Leave to stand for 2 minutes. Turn out into a serving dish and sprinkle chopped pistachio nuts over the surface. Sprinkle the liqueur over all and serve hot or warm.

SPICED BANANA MUFFINS WITH ORANGE BUTTER

These fruity muffins of somewhat unusual texture are delicious when eaten with a Cointreau-flavoured sweet butter mixture (see page 105). Make it first to have ready once the muffins have cooked.

Makes 12 muffins

50 g (2 oz) butter

1 medium banana, chopped

1 whole egg

1 egg yolk

50 g (2 oz) rolled oats

100 g (4 oz) soft brown sugar

10 ml (2 level tsp) ground cinnamon

5 ml (1 level tsp) baking powder

2.5 ml ($\frac{1}{2}$ level tsp) salt

100 g (4 oz) plain flour

1. In a medium heatproof bowl, microwave the butter, uncovered, on HIGH for 30 seconds until it melts. Stir in the chopped banana, whole egg and egg yolk and mix well.
2. Put the oats and sugar in a separate bowl, add the banana mixture and all the remaining ingredients sifted together. Stir quickly.
3. Use the mixture to half fill paper bun cases and microwave, 6 at a time, uncovered, on HIGH for 4–4$\frac{1}{2}$ minutes or until springy to the touch.
4. Leave to stand for at least 2 minutes before turning out and serving with the (previously made) Cointreau butter (page 105).

Stemmed glassful of Iced Kiwi Fruit Sabayon (page 117); Apricot Madeira Bombe (page 114).

Top: Cardamon Pecan Slices (page 107) with soured cream and chocolate curls.
Above left: Wedges of Passion Cake (page 106).
Above right: Wrapped Figs with Praline Butter (page 98).
Right: Cherry Preserve Fort Enda (page 94) on a pillow of creamy Greek yogurt.

Top to bottom: Pecan Brittle (page 121); Caramel with Sesame Seeds (page 120); Chocolate and Brazil Nut Fudge (page 121).

CHRISTMAS PUDDING

Do you usually leave everything to the last minute at Christmas? Well, here is a Christmas pudding you can make on the very day! It is prepared and cooked in minimal time, contains no flour and has a 'fresh fruit' taste. For the dried mixed fruit, use traditional raisins, sultanas and currants; for the dried fruit mixture use dried peach, banana, apricot, pear or apple. 'Trail mix' is available from health food shops and in this recipe provides novel texture contrasts. The whisky butter is for the stubbornly insouciant, who defy butter to harden their arteries.

Serves 8

25 g (1 oz) butter

75 g (3 oz) golden syrup

50 ml (2 fl oz) milk

1 egg

grated rind of 1 orange

100 g (4 oz) madeira cake crumbs

5 ml (1 level tsp) baking powder

5 ml (1 level tsp) cocoa

5 ml (1 level tsp) cinnamon

5 ml (1 level tsp) mixed spice

5 ml (1 level tsp) ground ginger

2.5 ml ($\frac{1}{2}$ level tsp) nutmeg

225 g (8 oz) dried mixed fruit

100 g (4 oz) dried fruit mixture

100 g (4 oz) dried 'trail mix'

Whisky Butter

45 ml (3 tbsp) whisky

50 g (2 oz) icing sugar

100 g (4 oz) softened butter

1. Base line a 900 ml (1$\frac{1}{2}$ pint) heatproof bowl using baking parchment.
2. Microwave the butter and golden syrup, uncovered, in another small heatproof bowl on HIGH for 40 seconds.
3. Add the milk, egg and orange rind. Beat well.
4. Sieve the dry ingredients into a large bowl and stir in the dried fruits.
5. Add the liquid egg mixture, mixing well together.
6. Spoon into the prepared bowl. Cover with baking parchment and microwave on HIGH for 7 minutes or until the centre is cooked.
7. Turn out and leave to stand for at least 15 minutes. Serve with whisky butter made by simply whisking the final 3 ingredients until they are light and fluffy. Chill briefly.

COINTREAU BUTTER

This mixture is something between an icing and a spread. It makes sufficient for 12 muffins, brioches or croissants and is also a delicious accompaniment for Christmas pudding and mince pies.

   Recipes such as these are for unabashed sybarites. Use this delicious butter for any warm breadstuff you please.

100 g (4 oz) unsalted butter

25 g (1 oz) icing sugar, sifted

30 ml (2 tbsp) Cointreau

1. To soften butter straight from the fridge, dice it into 1 cm ($\frac{1}{2}$ inch) cubes and place in a small heatproof bowl. Microwave, uncovered, on LOW (30%) for 40 seconds.
2. Add the icing sugar and Cointreau to the softened butter and beat well until light and fluffy. Serve a spoonful on top of each warm muffin, brioche or croissant.

PASSION CAKE

The origin of Passion Cake is unclear. Suffice it to say that carrots and spice of various kinds remain constant ingredients. This particular carrot cake recipe has a moist texture and a delightfully spicy taste. It cooks very well in the microwave and is enhanced by a delicious frosting of sharp, lemon-flavoured cream cheese. When serving, the pulp of a fresh passion fruit may be spooned over the frosting — and so further substantiate the name!

Serves 8–12

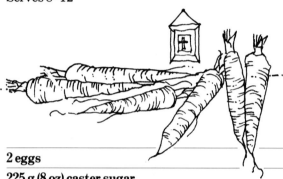

2 eggs
225 g (8 oz) caster sugar
175 ml (6 fl oz) oil
5 ml (1 tsp) vanilla essence
225 g (8 oz) carrot, finely grated
150 g (5 oz) flour
10 ml (2 level tsp) ground cinnamon
5 ml (1 level tsp) baking powder
2.5 ml (½ level tsp) salt

Frosting

175 g (6 oz) cream cheese
juice of 1 lemon
60 ml (4 level tbsp) icing sugar

Decoration (optional)

1 passion fruit

1. Base line a 23 cm (9 inch) microwave ring mould using baking parchment.
2. Beat the eggs, sugar, oil and vanilla essence in a large mixing bowl.
3. Add the carrot and sieve the remaining dry ingredients into the mixture before stirring. Do not over mix.
4. Spoon the mixture into the prepared dish and cover lightly with baking parchment. Microwave on HIGH for 8 minutes, rotating the dish after 4 minutes.
5. Leave to stand for 5 minutes, then turn out.
6. Make the frosting by beating the cheese, lemon juice and icing sugar together until the mixture is smooth and pliable and the flavours have blended. Allow the cake to cool before frosting, using a palette knife.
7. If wished, halve the passion fruit and spoon the pulp over the frosting.

See photograph page 102

CHOCOLATE BRAMBLE GÂTEAU

Cakes which rely solely on whisked eggs (and the air they contain) as their raising agent do not always work satisfactorily in microwave cookery. This attractive and delectable layered cake contains well-whisked eggs and some baking powder to keep the texture light. It also has berry purée folded both into the cake mixture itself, and into the pink 'marbled' cream between each layer, so giving a rich, moist texture.

Serves 6–8

100 g (4 oz) blackberries
10 ml (2 level tsp) icing sugar
3 eggs
75 g (3 oz) caster sugar
50 g (2 oz) plain flour
25 g (1 oz) cocoa
10 ml (2 level tsp) baking powder
15–30 ml (1–2 tbsp) Crème de Cacao (chocolate liqueur)

Decoration

300 ml (½ pint) double cream, chilled
50 g (2 oz) blackberries

1. Prepare 3 rectangular cake pans, 600 ml (1 pint) capacity each, by lightly greasing the sides and lining the base with non-stick paper.
2. Purée the blackberries with the icing sugar, using a food processor and sieve to remove the

seeds. Reserve 30 ml (2 level tbsp) of this sieved purée for later use.

3. Whisk together the eggs and sugar with an electric beater until they are light and fluffy and almost trebled in volume. (The mixture will leave a trail when beaters are lifted out.)

4. Sift together the flour, cocoa and baking powder and lightly fold it into the egg mixture in two stages. Fold in the blackberry purée, reserving 25 ml (1½ tbsp) for decoration.

5. Divide the mixture evenly between the 3 cake pans.

6. Position the cake pans evenly in the centre of the microwave oven. Microwave on MEDIUM for 5½–6 minutes, changing positions halfway through cooking time so that each pan is cooked evenly throughout.

7. Leave to stand for 5 minutes before turning out and sprinkling the chocolate liqueur over the cakes. Leave to cool.

8. Whip the chilled cream until it just holds its shape, then lightly stir the reserved purée through the cream for a marbled effect.

9. Cover each layer with the cream and sandwich together. Decorate with whole berries.

CARDAMOM PECAN SLICE

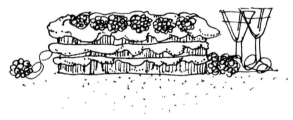

This spiced mixture has a firm texture and is best eaten fresh, preferably warm, with coffee, or as a dessert with whipped cream, ice cream or crème pâtisserie. When first removed from the oven, parts of the surface are damp or even wet in places. This is to be expected and further cooking is not recommended as the mixture will dry out and become unappetizing. Exact timing is essential for this recipe; residual heat will continue the cooking after the dish is removed from the oven.

Serves 6–8

150 g (5 oz) icing sugar
2 eggs
100 g (4 oz) butter
150 g (5 oz) plain flour
5 ml (1 level tsp) baking powder
50 g (2 oz) cocoa
10 ml (2 level tsp) powdered cardamom
5 ml (1 level tsp) ground cinnamon
50 g (2 oz) pecan nuts, chopped
45 ml (3 tbsp) brandy

1. Lightly grease and with baking parchment base line a 23 cm (9 inch) round microware flan or other straight-sided dish. Place a 7.5 cm (3 inch) round drinking glass in the centre. Alternatively, use a 23 cm (9 inch) microware ring mould.

2. Sift the icing sugar into a bowl. Add the eggs and whisk together for about 1–2 minutes or until the mixture is light and fluffy.

3. Put the butter in a heatproof bowl, loosely cover with cling film and microwave on HIGH for 1 minute. Sift the baking powder, flour, cocoa, cardamom and cinnamon together in a bowl.

4. Sift half the flour mixture over the egg mixture and fold in lightly. Pour in half the cooled butter, then gradually fold in the remaining flour and butter alternately. Stir in the nuts to form a batter. Do NOT over mix.

5. Spoon the mixture into the prepared dish and cover with baking parchment. Microwave on HIGH for 5 minutes. Remove from the oven and leave to stand in the baking dish. The edges will be very moist or even wet when first removed from the oven but the mixture continues to cook during standing time. Peel away the parchment and discard.

6. Turn the slice out, remove the base paper and sprinkle with brandy, or other liquor.

7. Dredge with icing sugar (it may form an unusual marbled effect from the pattern of the paper) and serve warm, cut into wedges.

See photograph page 102

───── COOK'S TIP ─────
If pecan nuts are unavailable, walnuts can be used, but will not give such an interesting result.

MAGIC MICROWAVE MERINGUES

Meringues made by the usual method simply do not work in a microwave oven. But meringues made by this totally different method have to be seen to be believed; they rise as if by magic from a solid, fondant-like ball to a snowy white puff of crispness. It is a novelty few can resist trying. Since the raw fondant-meringue mixture must be very dry, only a little egg white is used to a large volume of icing sugar. This small amount of mixture produces 24 meringues and a large, Pavlova-type meringue which can be stored for later use. Alternatively, you can make 48 meringues — good value for money! Use them crushed on fruit fools, folded into unsweetened coffee-flavoured cream as a dessert, or with after-dinner digestifs sandwiched together with cream.

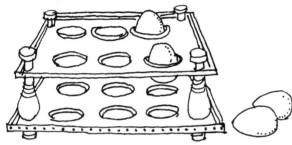

Makes 48 meringues, or 24 meringues and 1 large Pavlova

---

white of a size 6 egg (or $\frac{1}{2}$ the white of a size 3 egg)

250 g (9 oz) icing sugar

---

1. Place the egg white in a small bowl. Add the icing sugar and mix well, first using a spoon and then the hands to form a dry, pliable 'fondant'. Work well to incorporate all the icing sugar.

To make individual meringues
1. Roll small pieces of the fondant-meringue in the hands to form 1.25 cm ($\frac{1}{2}$ inch) balls. Arrange 12 balls, in 3 lines of 4, on a sheet of baking parchment or greaseproof paper.
2. Microwave on HIGH for 1 minute 30 seconds, without opening the door. Lift the cooked meringues off the paper and repeat the cooking procedure with the second batch of 12. To make 48 individual meringues, repeat and cook twice more.
3. If wished, divide the original fondant-meringue mixture in half to make 24 meringues and a large Pavlova.

To make a large Pavlova
1. Roll out half the mixture on a sheet of baking parchment or greaseproof paper into a 12.5 cm (5 inch) circle. Microwave on HIGH for 2 minutes without opening the door.
2. Remove from the paper and decorate with whipped cream and fresh fruit of your choice. Particularly delicious are sliced mango marinated in orange rind shreds and juice, or firm banana slices marinated in lime shreds and juice. Other ideas include substituting thick, Greek-type natural yogurt for the cream and spreading fresh pineapple with passion fruit pulp over the top.

CUSTARD SAUCE

Do you share my aversion to that garish yellow substance frequently served (in otherwise blameless establishments) as custard? The following recipe contains no eggs and can provide an honest solution to the 'quick cheap pudding' problem. It is served from the same vessel in which it is made. No burned saucepans and no spilled milk! For absolute indulgence, serve with baked apple, honeyed pear or peach halves.

Serves 4

---

25 g (1 oz) butter

45 ml (3 level tbsp) flour

225 ml (8 fl oz) milk

30 ml (2 level tbsp) caster sugar

5 ml (1 tsp) vanilla or almond essence

---

1. Put the butter into a medium heatproof bowl or jug. Cover and microwave on HIGH for 30 seconds or until melted.
2. Stir the flour into the butter until a smooth paste is formed. Microwave, uncovered, on HIGH for 30 seconds.
3. Whisk the milk and sugar into the butter and flour mixture, blending well. (The mixture may not be very smooth, in fact it looks alarmingly lumpy, but this phase passes.)
4. Microwave on HIGH for 1$\frac{1}{2}$ minutes, whisking every 30 seconds.
5. Stir in the vanilla or almond essence, according to choice, and serve hot.

DESSERTS, CAKES AND CUSTARDS

ICE-CREAM CUSTARD

The taste of this custard reminds me of ice-cream parlours and all their delights. Its final cooking stage is a little alarming, as the mixture bubbles up and appears to be curdled, or lumpy, or both. The mixture simply needs to be whisked thoroughly to become creamy-smooth. Coat individual servings with prepared fresh fruit such as bananas, kiwi fruit, mango or pawpaw.

Serves 4

40 g (1½ oz) butter

45 ml (3 level tbsp) cornflour

450 ml (15 fl oz) milk

2 eggs

45 ml (3 level tbsp) brown sugar

2.5 ml (½ tsp) Angostura bitters (optional)

1. Put the butter in a heatproof 900 ml (1½ pint) bowl and microwave, uncovered, on HIGH for 1 minute.
2. Add the cornflour and microwave, uncovered, on HIGH for a further 30 seconds.
3. In a separate heatproof bowl, beat a little of the milk with the eggs and sugar.
4. Add the remaining milk to the butter and flour and mix well. Microwave on HIGH for 4 minutes.
5. Whisk the hot sauce into the egg mixture, cover loosely with cling film and return to the microwave oven. Microwave on HIGH for 1 minute. Cool, stirring frequently.
6. Spoon into serving dishes and serve warm, cool or chilled.

CRÈME CARAMEL

If these instructions are scrupulously followed, a perfect, velvety and unblemished custard will be turned out of its dish. If any slight change is made, in timing or in dimensions of the container, then absolute success cannot be guaranteed and bubbles may form. As with many microwaved foods, custards seem to retain every last vestige of texture and taste of the original ingredients, so use the freshest eggs and the finest vanilla sugar.

Serves 4

Caramel

30 ml (2 level tbsp) caster sugar

60 ml (4 tbsp) water

Custard

350 ml (12 fl oz) creamy milk

15 ml (1 level tbsp) vanilla sugar

2 eggs, lightly whisked

1. Put the caster sugar and 10 ml (2 tsp) of the water into a straight-sided porcelain or heatproof glass soufflé dish. Microwave, uncovered, on HIGH for about 2 minutes or until it becomes straw coloured.
2. Add the remaining water and microwave on HIGH for 1½–2 minutes or until caramelised and the colour is a rich brown. Turn the dish 3 times during cooking.
3. Carefully remove the hot dish and allow it to stand while the caramel sets and cools slightly.
4. Put the milk and vanilla sugar into a heatproof glass measuring jug. Microwave, uncovered, on HIGH for 2 minutes. Stir well, checking that the sugar has dissolved.
5. Pour the milk onto the whisked eggs, then strain the custard mixture back into the prepared caramel-lined dish.
6. Microwave, covered loosely with cling film, on 30%/LOW for 8 minutes, giving the dish a quarter turn every 2 minutes. Then carefully remove the hot dish from the oven. At this stage the mixture looks definitely undercooked and semi-liquid in the centre, but the residual heat continues cooking the custard after it leaves the microwave oven.
7. Cover the dish with a double thickness of kitchen paper. If it is to be eaten hot or warm, leave to stand for at least 10 minutes.
8. If the caramel is to be turned out, leave it to stand as above, then refrigerate for at least 2 hours. Invert it in one rapid movement on to a serving dish.

SURPRISE CUSTARD

This simple recipe uses ingredients which, though unprepossessing, give a clean, old-fashioned taste to the custard. Serve it with sliced, fresh, seasonal fruit (dusted with vanilla sugar, a trickle of fruit liqueur, or rose or orange flower water). Topped with whipped cream and chopped nuts, it becomes a party pudding.

Serves 4

45 ml (3 level tbsp) cornflour
10 ml (2 level tsp) vanilla sugar
225 ml (8 fl oz) milk
15 g ($\frac{1}{2}$ oz) butter
30–60 ml (2–4 tbsp) single cream or creamy milk

1. In a medium heatproof bowl, combine the cornflour with the sugar.
2. Stir in the milk and add the butter, in small pieces, to the mixture. Microwave on HIGH for $2\frac{1}{2}$ minutes, uncovered, stirring halfway through cooking time. Allow to cool.
3. Depending on the consistency required, stir in a little cream or creamy milk to thin the custard, as it tends to thicken if allowed to stand.

Coffee Custard
Add 15 ml (1 level tbsp) instant coffee granules to 15 ml (1 tbsp) boiling water and stir in with the milk at stage 2. Serve chilled.

Praline Custard
Stir in 50 g (2 oz) powdered praline (page 121) to the finished custard. Serve chilled.

Malted Custard
Stir 45 ml (3 tbsp) liquid malt extract into the cooked custard. Serve warm or cool.

Chocolate Custard
Put 125 g (4 oz) plain chocolate in a heatproof bowl with 30 ml (2 tbsp) single cream or creamy milk. Microwave, uncovered, on HIGH for 2–$2\frac{1}{2}$ minutes, stir to mix and fold into the cooked custard. Serve cool or chilled.

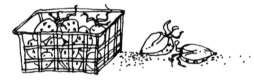

Strawberry Fool
Roughly crush 125 g (4 oz) hulled strawberries with 45 ml (3 level tbsp) icing sugar on a heatproof plate. Microwave on HIGH for 1 minute, or until the juice runs. Fold into the cooked custard. Serve chilled.

Raspberry Fool
Proceed as for strawberry fool, substituting raspberries for strawberries. Serve chilled.

I·C·E·S, S·O·R·B·E·T·S AND S·A·B·A·Y·O·N·S

CLASSIC VANILLA ICE-CREAM

This simple recipe can be used as the basis for any variation you may wish. It's also very good served plain with fruit, nuts or wafers of your choice.

Serves 4–6

120 ml (4 fl oz) water

25 g (1 oz) vanilla sugar

50 g (2 oz) caster sugar

3 egg yolks (at room temperature)

300 ml ($\frac{1}{2}$ pint) double cream, whipped

1. Mix together the water and both types of sugar in a 600 ml (1 pint) heatproof glass measuring jug and microwave on MEDIUM, uncovered, for 2 minutes to ensure that the sugar is dissolved. Stir the mixture thoroughly.
2. Microwave the syrup for a further 6 minutes, uncovered, on HIGH or until it forms a thick bubbling syrup. DO NOT STIR AT THIS STAGE. The temperature should reach 110°C (225°F).
3. Slightly cool the syrup, then pour it onto the egg yolks and whisk until light and fluffy.
4. Fold in the whipped cream and pour the mixture into a shallow freezeproof plastic container. Cover and seal.
5. Fast freeze until almost solid (2–3 hours).
6. Remove from the freezer and whisk the mixture until smooth. Re-freeze until firm (about 2 hours).
7. Soften slightly in the refrigerator before serving, or 'ripen' using the microwave for 15–20 seconds on HIGH, covered.

AVOCADO AND ORANGE ICE-CREAM

This mild-flavoured and simply delicious sweet can be served with twists of fresh orange.

Serves 4–6

120 ml (4 fl oz) water

25 g (1 oz) vanilla sugar

50 g (2 oz) caster sugar

3 egg yolks (at room temperature)

300 ml ($\frac{1}{2}$ pint) double cream, whipped

1 large ripe avocado, skinned, stoned and mashed

juice and grated rind of 1 orange

1. Mix together the water and both types of sugar in a 600 ml (1 pint) heatproof glass measuring jug and microwave on MEDIUM, uncovered, for 2 minutes to ensure that the sugar is dissolved. Stir the syrup mixture thoroughly.
2. Microwave for a further 6 minutes on HIGH, uncovered, until it forms a thick bubbling syrup. DO NOT STIR AT THIS STAGE. The temperature should reach 110°C (225°F).
3. Slightly cool the syrup then pour it onto the egg yolks and whisk until light and fluffy.
4. Fold in the whipped cream and pour the mixture into a shallow freezeproof plastic container. Cover and seal.
5. Fast freeze until almost solid (2–3 hours).
6. Remove from the freezer and whisk in the mashed avocado, orange juice and rind. Re-freeze until firm (about 1 hour).
7. Soften slightly in the refrigerator before serving, or 'ripen' using the microwave for 15–20 seconds on HIGH, uncovered.

TRUFFLED ICE-CREAM WITH COGNAC

Follow the recipe for homemade truffles (page 120) or else use the shop-bought variety for this rich confection. Serve in tiny iced dishes or glasses and follow with really good strong coffee and liqueurs for the perfect ending to a special meal.

Serves 6

100 ml (4 fl oz) water

25 g (1 oz) vanilla sugar

50 g (2 oz) caster sugar

3 egg yolks (at room temperature)

300 ml ($\frac{1}{2}$ pint) double cream, whipped

100 g (4 oz) Cognac truffles, chopped (page 120)

30 ml (2 tbsp) Cognac or brandy

1. Mix together the water and both types of sugar in a 600 ml (1 pint) heatproof glass measuring jug and microwave on MEDIUM, uncovered, for 2 minutes to ensure that the sugar is dissolved. Stir the mixture thoroughly.
2. Microwave the syrup for a further 6 minutes on HIGH, uncovered, or until it forms a thick bubbling syrup. DO NOT STIR AT THIS STAGE. The temperature should reach 110°C (225°F).
3. Slightly cool the syrup, then pour it onto the egg yolks and whisk until light and fluffy.
4. Fold in the double whipped cream and pour the mixture into a shallow, freezeproof plastic container. Cover and seal.
5. Fast freeze until almost solid (2–3 hours).
6. Remove from the freezer and stir in the chopped truffles and liqueur. Re-freeze until firm (about 1 hour).
7. Soften slightly in the refrigerator before serving, or 'ripen' using the microwave for 15–20 seconds on HIGH, covered.

COFFEE AND TOFFEE ICE-CREAM

Rich and wickedly voluptuous, this ice-cream has a lushness hard to explain in words. Treat yourself to it soon in order to remember the excellence of homemade ice-cream.

Serves 4–6

Toffee

50 g (2 oz) caster sugar

Ice-cream

3 eggs (at room temperature)

100 g (4 oz) icing sugar

15 ml (1 level tbsp) instant coffee granules

15 ml (1 tbsp) hot water

250 ml (8 fl oz) double cream

1. To make the toffee, cover a 20 cm (8 inch) browning dish with an even layer of caster sugar. Microwave on HIGH, uncovered, for 2 minutes or until the sugar melts, becoming a rich brown.
2. Holding the dish carefully with an oven glove, pour the toffee onto a lightly-oiled sheet of foil and leave to set (about 5 minutes). Remove from the foil and break into fragments.
3. Put the eggs and icing sugar into a deep, medium bowl and, using an electric beater, whisk until thick and mousse-like.
4. Dissolve the coffee in the hot water and add to the cream. Whip until soft but not too stiff. Fold the cream and egg mixtures together and turn into a shallow, freezeproof plastic container.
5. Cover, seal and fast freeze for 1$\frac{1}{2}$ hours. Push the toffee fragments into the surface, then cover, seal and re-freeze for a further 2 hours.
6. Serve straight from the freezer, accompanied by tuiles if wished.

AMARETTO GRANITA

I think Isabella Beeton would have approved of this: it has her style, though she would have used orgeat, not our 20th-century Amaretto liqueur. The effect is much the same: a shock of icy crystals and a whiff of almond to cleanse the palate between courses.

Serves 4

---

100 g (4 oz) caster sugar

600 ml (1 pint) water

finely grated rind and juice of 2 lemons

45 ml (3 tbsp) Amaretto or other almond-flavoured liqueur

25 g (1 oz) chopped almonds

---

1. Put the sugar, water and lemon rind in a medium heatproof bowl and microwave on HIGH for 2 minutes. Stir, then microwave on HIGH for a further 2 minutes.
2. Cool over ice, add the lemon juice and liqueur.
3. Pour into a shallow freezeproof plastic container and fast freeze for 2 hours or until frozen to a slush.
4. Whisk, using an electric beater, and return to the freezer, covered and sealed.
5. To serve, 'ripen' using the microwave for 15–20 seconds on HIGH, covered. Stir until crumbly, add chopped almonds and spoon into stemmed glasses.

POIRE WILLIAM SORBET

Crumbly textured and scented with pear, this sorbet can be eaten between courses or at the end of the meal as dessert, served with paper-thin chocolate wafers. The Poire William specified here is the world famed eau-de-vie and should never be mistaken for the insipid, over sweet liqueurs sold under similar names.

Serves 4

---

450 ml (15 fl oz) sweet white wine

75 g (3 oz) caster sugar

450 g (1 lb) William Bon Chrétien pears

45 ml (3 level tbsp) Poire William eau-de-vie

1 egg white

---

1. Put the wine and sugar into a medium heatproof bowl, cover and microwave on HIGH for 3 minutes. Cool the syrup over ice.
2. Peel, core and cube the pears and put into a shallow heatproof dish. Sprinkle with 2 tablespoons of the partly cooled syrup and microwave, uncovered, on HIGH for 2½–3 minutes. Mash or purée until smooth.
3. Add the Poire William and cooled syrup. Turn into a shallow freezeproof plastic container. Cover, seal and fast freeze for 2 hours or until frozen to a slush. Crush using a food processor or electric beater.
4. Whisk the egg white until stiff peaks form, and fold into the sorbet.
5. Cover, seal and freeze until firm (about 2 hours).
6. 'Ripen' using the microwave for 30 seconds on HIGH, covered.
7. Stir until crumbly, spoon into tall glasses and serve immediately.

MALIBU COCONUT ICE

Coconut toasts admirably in the microwave and its chewy texture is particularly good when combined with a complementary liqueur.

Serves 4

50 g (2 oz) desiccated coconut
120 ml (4 fl oz) water
25 g (1 oz) vanilla sugar
50 g (2 oz) caster sugar
3 egg yolks
300 ml (½ pint) double cream, whipped
60 ml (4 tbsp) Malibu or other coconut-flavoured liqueur

1. Spread the desiccated coconut in a shallow heatproof dish and microwave, uncovered, on HIGH for 3 minutes, stirring halfway through cooking time.
2. Mix together the water and both types of sugar in a 600 ml (1 pint) measuring jug and microwave on MEDIUM, uncovered, for 2 minutes to ensure that the sugar is dissolved. Stir the mixture thoroughly.
3. Microwave the syrup for a further 6 minutes on HIGH, uncovered, or until it forms a thick bubbling syrup. DO NOT STIR AT THIS STAGE. The temperature should reach 110°C (225°F).
4. Slightly cool the syrup, then pour it onto the egg yolks and whisk until light and fluffy. Cool over ice.
5. Fold in the double whipped cream and pour the mixture into a shallow, freezeproof plastic container. Cover and seal.
6. Freeze until almost solid (2–3 hours).
7. Whisk in the toasted coconut and the liqueur until the mixture is smooth. Re-freeze until firm (about 1½ hours).
8. Soften slightly in the refrigerator before serving, or 'ripen' using the microwave for 15–20 seconds on HIGH, covered.

APRICOT MADEIRA BOMBE

In classic cookery, the form of a particular food (as well as its taste, aroma, colour and texture) significantly contributed to its appeal. For me this is still a pleasurable ideal, and one which is exploited in this recipe. Scoops of this ice-cream would taste the same but seem less inviting. As it is, the elegant dome can be covered with piped cream and decorated with angelica, cut into shapes.

Serves 6–8

225 g (8 oz) dried apricots
150 ml (¼ pint) Madeira or other fortified wine
3 egg yolks (at room temperature)
100 g (4 oz) soft brown sugar
300 ml (½ pint) single cream
300 ml (½ pint) double cream, whipped

Decoration (optional)

15 g (½ oz) angelica, cut into slivers
reserved whipped cream

1. Put the apricots and Madeira in a medium heatproof bowl and microwave, covered, for 4 minutes on HIGH. Purée in a blender or food processor, cool over ice and set aside.
2. Whisk together the egg yolks and brown sugar until very thick.
3. Pour the single cream into a heatproof bowl and microwave, uncovered, on HIGH for 2 minutes.
4. Pour the single cream onto the egg mixture and blend thoroughly.
5. Place the bowl of mixture into a larger bowl

containing hot water. (The hot water should be at the same level as the mixture.) Microwave, lightly covered, on LOW for 10 minutes, stirring 3 times.

6. Cool the mixture over ice then fold in the whipped double cream, reserving some for decoration.

7. Pour the mixture into a shallow freezeproof plastic container, cover and seal. Freeze until almost solid (2–3 hours).

8. Remove from the freezer and whisk in the apricot purée. Turn into a 1.2 litre (2 pint) bombe mould. Cover and re-freeze until firm.

9. To serve, dip the container into tepid water and turn its contents out onto a chilled serving plate. Smooth the surface if necessary and re-freeze for 10 minutes. Decorate with reserved whipped cream and angelica if wished.

See photograph page 101

BROWN BREAD AND ALMOND TORTONI

This luxurious, loaf-shaped parfait has a touch of Edwardian grandeur about its name. But it is very much a 'time-warp' recipe, as the microwave oven of the 1980s makes the dish quick to prepare and the drudgery disappears along with the washing up. Offer a delicious Muscat de Beaumes de Venise or a good Sauternes to your guests with this dessert.

Serves 4–6

Bread Caramel

75 g (3 oz) wholemeal breadcrumbs

50 g (2 oz) toasted almonds

50 g (2 oz) muscovado sugar

Custard Cream

3 egg yolks (at room temperature)

100 g (4 oz) soft brown sugar

300 ml ($\frac{1}{2}$ pint) single cream

300 ml ($\frac{1}{2}$ pint) double cream, whipped

1. Combine the breadcrumbs, toasted almonds and muscovado sugar in a browning dish. (There

is no need to pre-heat the dish.)

2. Microwave on HIGH for 3 minutes, stirring halfway through cooking time. Leave to cool.

3. Use a food processor to break down the larger pieces, or crush with a rolling pin.

4. Whisk together the egg yolks and brown sugar until very thick.

5. Put the single cream into a heatproof bowl and microwave, uncovered, on HIGH for 2 minutes.

6. Pour the single cream onto the egg mixture and mix thoroughly until combined.

7. Place the bowl of mixture inside a larger bowl containing hot water. (The hot water should be at the same level as the mixture.) Microwave on LOW for 10 minutes, loosely covered, stirring 3 times.

8. Cool over ice, then fold in the whipped double cream.

9. Pour the mixture into a freezeproof plastic loaf dish, cover and seal. Freeze until almost solid (2 hours).

10. Remove from the freezer and whisk in the caramelised bread and nut mixture. Re-freeze until firm (about 2 hours).

11. Soften slightly in the refrigerator before serving, or 'ripen' using the microwave for 20–25 seconds on HIGH, covered. Turn out onto a chilled serving dish and serve sliced.

MERINGUE AND STRAWBERRY MOULDED MOUSSE

This frozen mousse combines interesting textures and tastes. The berries are softened in the microwave to develop flavour and the gelatine is melted in the oven before being added.

Serves 8

450 g (1 lb) ripe strawberries, hulled and halved
100 g (4 oz) caster sugar
15 ml (1 tbsp) lemon juice, freshly squeezed
2 eggs (at room temperature)
15 g ($\frac{1}{2}$ oz) powdered gelatine
45 ml (3 tbsp) cold water
300 ml ($\frac{1}{2}$ pint) double cream
100 g (4 oz) meringues, crushed

1. Reserve 8 good strawberry halves for decoration and put the rest into a shallow heatproof casserole with just 25 g (1 oz) of the caster sugar. Crush with a fork and sprinkle with lemon juice. Loosely cover with cling film and microwave on HIGH for 1 minute, or until the juices run. Mash again and leave to cool.
2. Break the eggs into a medium bowl, add the remaining 75 g (3 oz) of caster sugar and whisk using an electric beater until the mixture becomes thick and mousse-like.
3. Stir the gelatine into the water in a heatproof cup and leave to soak until firm. Microwave, covered, on HIGH for 1 minute, or until melted. Mix into the strawberry purée.
4. Whip the cream until it forms soft peaks. Reserve a little for decoration.
5. Fold the almost setting strawberry-gelatine mixture into the egg mixture with the cream and crushed meringues.
6. Turn into a lightly oiled 1.75 litre (3 pint) freezeproof fluted ring mould, cover with foil, seal and leave to set. Freeze until firm (about 2 hours).
7. Stand the mould briefly in cool water then invert onto a serving dish. Decorate with reserved berries and cream.

BANANA AND BACARDI PARFAIT

I wanted to call this confection 'cocktail parfait' but my husband, who loathes most cocktails, felt the title might deter an intending cook. So be it. I leave it for you to decide the suitability or otherwise of my choice.

Serves 4–6

3 egg yolks (at room temperature)
100 g (4 oz) soft dark brown sugar
300 ml ($\frac{1}{2}$ pint) single cream
300 ml ($\frac{1}{2}$ pint) double cream, whipped
2 large ripe bananas, peeled and mashed
45 ml (3 level tbsp) Bacardi or other light rum

1. Whisk together the egg yolks and brown sugar until very thick.
2. Put the single cream into a heatproof bowl and microwave, uncovered, for 2 minutes on HIGH.
3. Pour the single cream onto the egg mixture and combine thoroughly.
4. Place the bowl of mixture into another larger bowl containing hot water. (The hot water should reach the same level as the mixture.) Microwave on LOW for 10 minutes, loosely covered.
5. Cool the mixture over ice, then fold in the double whipped cream.
6. Pour the mixture into a shallow freezeproof plastic container, cover and seal. Fast freeze until almost solid (2–3 hours).
7. Remove from the freezer and whisk in the mashed banana and Bacardi. Re-freeze until firm, about 1$\frac{1}{2}$–2 hours.
8. Soften slightly in the refrigerator before serving, or 'ripen' using the microwave for 20–25 seconds on HIGH, covered. Serve in parfait dishes with crisp wafers.

ICED KIWI FRUIT SABAYON

Cooking kiwi fruit according to this recipe results in a golden, seeded purée with a delicate but less astringent taste than when used raw. Lime rind and juice add a certain sharpness, and the traditional Marsala is replaced by vodka. Not a recipe for traditionalists!

Serves 4

4 large kiwi fruit, about 350 g (12 oz)
100 g (4 oz) icing sugar
60 ml (4 tbsp) water
grated rind and juice of 1 lime
30 ml (2 tbsp) vodka
4 egg yolks (at room temperature)
250 ml (8 fl oz) whipping cream

Decoration (optional)

fresh kiwi fruit slices

1. Skin the kiwi fruit and cut the flesh into 1 cm (½ inch) cubes. Put into a medium heatproof bowl, cover loosely with cling film and microwave on HIGH for 2 minutes. Purée using a fork.
2. Put the icing sugar and water in a medium heatproof bowl and microwave, uncovered, on HIGH for 2 minutes. Stir and microwave on HIGH for a further 1 minute. Cool the syrup over ice, then stir in the purée, the lime rind and juice and the vodka.
3. Add 2 tablespoons of this mixture to the egg yolks. Whisk, using an electric beater, until thick and mousse-like, adding the remaining mixture gradually.
4. Lightly whip the cream and fold in. Turn into a shallow freezeproof container, then cover, seal and fast freeze for 2½–3 hours, or until firm.
5. Serve scoops of the iced sabayon with slices of fresh kiwi fruit if wished.

See photograph page 101

SOUTH SEAS SABAYON

This layered warm dessert reminds me of French colonial outposts like Tahiti where liquor and tropical fruit seem to abound, and colours are so vivid. Using the microwave, it is so quick to cook that it can be made between courses with only a little advance preparation of the pawpaw. Enjoy it still warm with crisp biscuits.

Serves 4

350 g (12 oz) fresh pawpaw
15 ml (1 tbsp) freshly squeezed lime juice
3 egg yolks
75 g (3 oz) caster sugar
45 ml (3 tbsp) Calvados, Applejack or brandy
4 or 8 langue de chat, or wafer biscuits

1. Remove the skin, halve and then seed the pawpaw (there should be about 225 g [8 oz] weight of prepared flesh). Slice the pawpaw thinly on to a shallow heatproof plate or dish and sprinkle with the lime juice.
2. Microwave, uncovered, on HIGH for 3 minutes, stirring from edges to centre halfway through cooking time. Using a fork, mash the cooked fruit to a rough pulp and set aside.
3. Put the egg yolks, sugar and Calvados into a medium heatproof bowl, stirring together thoroughly. Microwave, uncovered, for 20 seconds or until just barely warm.
4. Using a hand-held electric beater or rotary whisk, whisk the lukewarm sabayon mixture continuously until it becomes pale, very thick and has tripled in volume.
5. Arrange layers of the warm fruit pulp and the warm sabayon alternately in heatproof serving goblets.

D·R·I·N·K·S AND S·W·E·E·T·M·E·A·T·S

SCENTED ORANGE TEA WITH CIDER

Tea forms the basis of this sustaining light punch and as the quality of the tea determines the final flavour, scented teas are advised. The Orange Amère specified here is a discovery I made in Paris: it comes from the premises of Mariage Frères, Rue de Cloitre, St Merri, Paris.

Serves 1

150 ml (¼ pint) **strong tea such as Orange Amère or Earl Grey**

150 ml (¼ pint) **medium cider**

15 ml (1 level tbsp) **honey**

7.5 cm (3 inch) **strip thinly pared orange rind**

3 **cloves**

15 ml (1 level tbsp) **dark rum or whisky**

1. Strain the tea into a large heatproof glass, glass mug or china mug.
2. Add the cider, honey and strip of orange rind stuck with the cloves. Cover with cling film.
3. Microwave on HIGH for 1 minute, or until very hot and steaming.
4. Stir in the spirit of your choice and sip while the tea is still hot. Alternatively, in hot weather, splash it on to lots of ice in a tall glass for a refreshing cool drink.

HOT JUCALETTE VELVET NIGHTCAP

In Samuel Pepys's time, partaking of chocolate or 'jucalette', as he called it, was thought to be a new and delectable vice. Hot chocolate, it was surmised, had stimulating propensities! This recipe certainly is wickedly calorific and rather alcoholic, but quite noteworthy.

Serves 4

90 g (3½ oz) **bar of good quality plain chocolate**

450 ml (15 fl oz) **creamy milk**

30 ml (2 tbsp) **granulated sugar**

2.5 ml (½ level tsp) **instant coffee granules**

1.25 ml (¼ tsp) **ground cinnamon**

60 ml (4 tbsp) **'Black Velvet' rye whiskey**

Topping

150 ml (¼ pint) **whipping cream, whisked until frothy**

1 cm (½ inch) **cinnamon stick, finely shredded (optional)**

1. Put the chocolate into a deep heatproof bowl and microwave, uncovered, on HIGH for 2 minutes or until melted.
2. Whisk in the milk, sugar, coffee and cinnamon. Microwave, uncovered, on HIGH for 4½ minutes. Stir well.
3. To serve, spoon a quarter of the whiskey into each of the 4 heatproof glasses or mugs and pour in the chocolate mixture. Slowly pour some whisked cream on top of each glass and sprinkle with the cinnamon shreds if wished. (Chewing and swallowing finely shredded cinnamon bark is perfectly enjoyable.) Drink while hot.

GARY'S COVENT GARDEN COMFORTER

Last November I visited London's new Covent Garden fruit and vegetable market at Nine Elms at 4 o'clock in the morning. A friend, an accomplished buyer from a famous store, acted as my guide, and after an exhaustive (but successful) search for perfect photogenic strawberries we retired to the bar. This is what I drank, along with the locals, some of whom had been playing snooker next door at the end of a hard day's night.

Serves 1

150 ml (¼ pint) creamy milk
a little nutmeg, freshly grated
15 ml (1 level tbsp) caster sugar
60 ml (4 tbsp) brandy, whisky or dark rum

1. Put the milk, nutmeg and sugar into a very large heatproof glass goblet or jug. Microwave, uncovered, on HIGH for 2 minutes.
2. Add your chosen spirit, stir and savour this most comforting of beverages.

RED RUIN

This hot cocktail brings a pleasant euphoria to all who dare drink it. Covering it with pierced cling film while it heats keeps the alcohol content fairly intact. Remove this cover just before drinking and savour the warming fumes.

Serves 1–2

90 ml (6 tbsp) dry vermouth
30 ml (2 tbsp) campari
15 ml (1 tbsp) sirop de groseilles (redcurrant syrup)
5 ml (1 tsp) lime juice cordial
30 ml (2 tbsp) white wine
10 cm (4 inch) stem of fresh borage
10 cm (4 inch) mint sprig
2 orange segments with peel
15 ml (1 tbsp) gin

1. Put all the liquid ingredients except the gin into a heatproof glass or mug. Add the herbs and orange segments. Cover with cling film, pierced in 2 places.
2. Microwave on HIGH for 1½ minutes until hot. Carefully remove the pierced cling film, add the gin, stir and serve immediately.

HURST'S PUNCH

One of Edward Lear's nonsense rhymes begins:

> *'There was an old person of Hurst*
> *Who drank when he was not athirst'*

One must presume, therefore, that it was purely for enjoyment's sake. This restorative and convivial punch should be consumed for similar reasons, and is good served warm (7 minutes) or very hot (9 minutes). The presence of lager is not merely fortuitous; it contributes to a very good taste indeed.

Serves 6–8

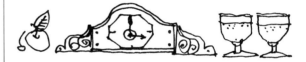

450 ml (15 fl oz) lager
600 ml (1 pint) unsweetened apple juice
1 red-skinned eating apple, cored and sliced into rings
10 cm (4 inch) cinnamon stick, flaked
10 allspice berries, lightly crushed
75 ml (5 tbsp) golden rum
120 ml (4 fl oz) Calvados or brandy

1. Put the lager, apple juice, sliced apple, cinnamon and allspice berries into a large, heatproof bowl or large punch bowl.
2. Microwave, uncovered, on HIGH for 7–9 minutes, according to preference.
3. Stir in the golden rum and Calvados and serve immediately in stemmed, heatproof goblets or mugs.

COGNAC TRUFFLES

Luxurious yet effortless, why has this simple recipe for self-indulgence not been created before? Keep and serve these tasty morsels chilled, for they quickly deteriorate when warm.

Makes 36

175 g (6 oz) plain chocolate
50 g (2 oz) butter
100 g (4 oz) madeira cake crumbs
30 ml (2 tbsp) double cream
1 egg yolk
30–45 ml (2–3 tbsp) Cognac (or rum)
100 g (4 oz) brazil nuts, finely chopped or food processed

1. Place the chocolate in a medium heatproof bowl. Microwave, uncovered, on HIGH for $2\frac{1}{2}$ minutes to melt.
2. Stir in small pieces of the butter, the fine madeira cake crumbs, double cream, egg yolk and Cognac. In a food processor, beat well until smooth and thick (2 minutes).
3. Chill until firm (about 45 minutes) and form into small balls. Roll each in ground or chopped brazil nuts.
4. Serve in tiny petits fours paper cases.

—— **SERVING TIP** ——
Serve at the end of a light meal in place of dessert, followed by a tiny iced glass of your favourite liqueur.

CARAMEL WITH SESAME SEEDS

Use oiled kitchen scissors to cut this chewy caramel while it is still warm, or else it may be hard to break cleanly later on.

Makes 36 pieces or 700 g ($1\frac{1}{2}$ lb)

50 g (2 oz) toasted sesame seeds (see below)
150 g (5 oz) sugar
150 g (5 oz) butter
400 g (14 oz) can sweetened condensed milk
5 ml (1 tsp) vanilla essence

1. Use foil to base line a 30 cm (6 inch) shallow, square cake tin. Oil lightly and sprinkle half the sesame seeds evenly over the base.
2. Place the remaining ingredients in a large heatproof bowl and microwave, uncovered, on HIGH for 10 minutes, stirring twice during cooking.
3. Beat vigorously with a wooden spoon until the mixture is smooth and golden brown in colour and then pour into the prepared tin. Sprinkle over and press in the rest of the sesame seeds.
4. Mark into small squares while still warm and use oiled scissors to cut into 'cushion-shaped' pieces. When cold, remove the squares of foil and wrap the caramel pieces individually in waxed paper or cellophane.

See photograph page 104

TOASTED SESAME SEEDS

Sesame seeds take much longer to toast than desiccated coconut, but the effect is similar. They continue to colour slightly after being removed from the microwave oven. Use them with confectionery, salads or oriental dishes.

50 g (2 oz) sesame seeds

1. Sprinkle the sesame seeds evenly over a shallow heatproof dish and microwave, uncovered, for 8 minutes, stirring from edge to centre every 2 minutes.

PECAN BRITTLE AND PRALINE

Peanut brittle always brings back memories of faded, kind and genteel maiden aunts who kept such homemade treats in store for young visitors like my sisters and me. It is a tradition fast dying out.

This brittle combines a butterscotch taste with pecan nuts. In chunks, it proves a child's delight, and powdered as praline it is very good indeed added to ice creams, folded into cream and custard and used as a topping on fruit desserts.

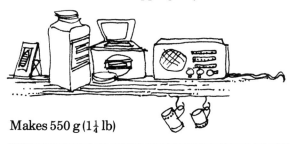

Makes 550 g (1¼ lb)

250 g (9 oz) granulated sugar
90 ml (6 tbsp) golden syrup
250 g (9 oz) pecan nuts
15 g (½ oz) butter
5 ml (1 level tsp) baking powder

1. Put the sugar and golden syrup in a large heat-proof bowl. Stir together. Microwave, uncovered, on HIGH for 4 minutes.
2. Stir in the pecan nuts and butter and micro-wave for a further 4 minutes on HIGH.
3. Sprinkle on the baking powder and then carefully stir it into the mixture until it bubbles up to become very light and frothy.
4. Pour on to a 50 cm (20 inch) length of lightly-oiled foil or greaseproof paper and leave to set. Tap sharply to break up the brittle into smallish pieces.
5. Store in an airtight container, each piece wrapped in waxed paper, foil, or cellophane.
6. To make pecan praline, use a toffee hammer or other blunt, heavy instrument to break the wrapped brittle into a coarse powder, or use a powerful food processor.

See photograph page 104

CHOCOLATE AND BRAZIL NUT FUDGE

A cheat's fudge, this one, but so very quick (two minutes) and luscious in flavour that it thoroughly earns its inclusion here. Really easy to make and with such predictably excellent results each time, it becomes the perfect candidate for school fêtes, last-minute Christmas gift parcels and, above all, for use in place of dessert with a strong black coffee.

Makes 36–49 pieces or 800 g (1¾ lb)

450 g (1 lb) icing sugar
50 g (2 oz) cocoa
pinch of salt
60 ml (4 tbsp) milk
100 g (4 oz) butter, cut into pieces
175 g (6 oz) brazil nuts, roughly chopped

1. Base line and lightly oil a 30–32 cm (6–7 inch) square cake tin. Sieve the icing sugar, cocoa and salt into a large heatproof bowl. Stir in the milk and then the butter pieces.
2. Microwave, uncovered, on HIGH for 2 minutes, then beat vigorously with a wooden spoon until smooth.
3. Sprinkle half the roughly chopped brazil nuts into the base of the prepared tin, then quickly pour the fudge mixture over. Sprinkle with the remaining nuts and leave to set. Mark and cut into 2.5 cm (1 inch) squares, as the mixture is a rich one. Wrap individually if wished and store in an airtight container.

See photograph page 104

U·S·E·F·U·L C·H·A·R·T·S

MEAT

Type	Time/Setting	Microwave Cooking Technique(s)
BEEF		
Boned roasting joint (sirloin, topside)	per 450 g (1 lb) Rare: 5–6 minutes on HIGH Medium: 7–8 minutes on HIGH Well: 8–10 minutes on HIGH	*Turn* joint over halfway through cooking time. *Stand* for 15–20 minutes tented with foil.
On the bone roasting joint (fore rib, back rib)	per 450 g (1 lb) Rare: 5 minutes on HIGH Medium: 6 minutes on HIGH Well: 8 minutes on HIGH	*Shield* bone end with small piece of foil during first half cooking time. *Turn* joint over halfway through cooking time. *Stand* as for boned joint.
LAMB/VEAL		
Boned rolled joint (loin, leg, shoulder)	per 450 g (1 lb) Medium: 7–8 minutes on HIGH Well: 8–10 minutes on HIGH	*Turn* joint over halfway through cooking time. *Stand* as for beef.
On the bone (leg and shoulder)	per 450 g (1 lb) Medium: 6–7 minutes on HIGH Well: 8–9 minutes on HIGH	*Shield* as for beef. *Position* fatty side down and turn over halfway through cooking time. *Stand* as for beef.
Crown roast of lamb	9–10 minutes on MEDIUM per 450 g (1 lb) stuffed weight	*Shield* bone tips with foil and overwrap with cling film. *Reposition* partway through cooking time. *Stand* for 20 minutes with foil tenting.
Chops	1½ minutes on HIGH, then 1½–2 minutes on MEDIUM	*Cook* in preheated browning dish, or finish off under grill. *Position* with bone ends towards centre.
PORK		
Boned rolled joint (loin, leg)	8–10 minutes on HIGH per 450 g (1 lb)	As for boned rolled lamb above.
On the bone (leg, hand)	8–9 minutes on HIGH per 450 g (1 lb)	As for lamb on the bone above.
Chops	1 chop: 4–4½ minutes on HIGH 2 chops: 5–5½ minutes on HIGH 3 chops: 6–7 minutes on HIGH 4 chops: 6½–8 minutes on HIGH	*Cook* in preheated browning dish, or finish off under grill. *Position* with bone ends towards centre. *Cover* kidney, if attached, with greaseproof paper. *Stand* for 2 minutes for 1 chop, 3–5 minutes for 2–4 chops.

Type	Time/Setting	Microwave Cooking Technique(s)
Sausages	2 sausages: 2½ minutes on HIGH 4 sausages: 4 minutes on HIGH	*Pierce* skins. *Cook* in preheated browning dish or finish off under grill. *Turn* occasionally during cooking.

BACON

Type	Time/Setting	Microwave Cooking Technique(s)
Joints	12–14 minutes on HIGH per 450 g (1 lb)	*Cook* in pierced roasting bag. *Turn* joint over partway through cooking time. *Stand* for 10 minutes, tented in foil.
Rashers	2 rashers: 2–2½ minutes on HIGH 4 rashers: 4–4½ minutes on HIGH 6 rashers: 5–6 minutes on HIGH 12 minutes on HIGH per 450 g (1 lb)	*Arrange* in a single layer. *Cover* with greaseproof paper to prevent splattering. *Cook* in preheated browning dish if preferred. *Remove* paper immediately after cooking to prevent sticking. For large quantities: *Overlap* slices and place on microwave rack. *Reposition* three times during cooking.

OFFAL

Type	Time/Setting	Microwave Cooking Technique(s)
Liver (lamb and calves)	6–8 minutes on HIGH per 450 g (1 lb)	*Cover* with greaseproof paper to prevent splattering.
Kidneys	8 minutes on HIGH per 450 g (1 lb)	*Arrange* in a circle. *Cover* to prevent splattering. *Reposition* during cooking.
Tongue	20 minutes on HIGH per 450 g (1 lb)	*Reposition* during cooking.

POULTRY

Type	Time/Setting	Microwave Cooking Technique(s)
CHICKEN		
Whole chicken	8–10 minutes on HIGH per 450 g (1 lb)	*Cook* in a roasting bag, breast side down and turn halfway through cooking. *Brown* under conventional grill, if preferred. *Stand* for 10–15 minutes.
Whole poussin	5 minutes on HIGH	*Cook* in a pierced roasting bag. *Turn* over as for whole chicken.

Type	Time/Setting	Microwave Cooking Technique(s)
Portions	6–8 minutes on HIGH per 450 g (1 lb)	*Position* skin side up with thinner parts towards centre. *Reposition* halfway through cooking time. *Stand* for 5–10 minutes.
Boneless breast	2–3 minutes on HIGH	*Brown* under grill, if preferred.

DUCK

Whole	7–10 minutes on HIGH per 450 g (1 lb)	*Turn* over as for whole chicken. *Stand* for 10–15 minutes.
Portions	4×300 g (11 oz) pieces: 10 minutes on HIGH, then 30–35 minutes on MEDIUM	*Position* and *reposition* as for chicken portions above.

TURKEY

Whole	9–11 minutes on HIGH per 450 g (1 lb)	*Turn* over 3–4 times, depending on size, during cooking; start cooking breast side down. *Stand* for 10–15 minutes.
Boneless roll	10 minutes on HIGH per 450 g (1 lb)	*Turn* over halfway through cooking time.

FISH

Type	Time/Setting	Microwave Cooking Technique(s)
Whole round fish (whiting, mullet, trout, carp, bream, small haddock)	3 minutes on HIGH per 450 g (1 lb)	*Slash* skin to prevent bursting. *Turn* over fish partway through cooking time. *Shield* tail with small pieces of smooth foil. *Reposition* fish if cooking more than 2.
Whole flat fish (plaice, sole)	3 minutes on HIGH	*Slash* skin. *Turn* dish partway through cooking time. *Shield* tail as for round fish.
Cutlets, steaks, fillets	4 minutes on HIGH per 450 g (1 lb)	*Position* thicker parts towards outside overlapping thin ends and separating with cling film. *Turn* over fillets and quarter-turn dish 3 times during cooking.
Smoked fish	4 minutes on HIGH per 450 g (1 lb)	Follow techniques for type of fish above.

RICE AND PASTA

Type and quantity	Time on HIGH	Microwave Cooking Technique(s)
White long grain rice 225 g (8 oz)	10–12 minutes	*Stir* once during cooking. *Stand* for 10 minutes.
Brown rice, 100 g (4 oz)	30 minutes	As for white long grain.
Pasta shapes, 225 g (8 oz) dried	7 minutes	*Stir* once during cooking. *Stand* for 5 minutes.
Spaghetti, tagliatelle, 225 g (8 oz) dried	7–8 minutes	*Stand* for 10 minutes.

FRESH VEGETABLES

Note: All times are given as a guide only, since variations in size and quality will affect cooking times. Add 30 ml (2 tbsp) water and cover unless otherwise stated.

Vegetable	Quantity	Approximate time on HIGH setting	Microwave Cooking Technique(s)
Artichoke, globe	1 2 3	5–6 minutes 7–8 minutes 11–12 minutes	*Place* upright in covered dish.
Asparagus	350 g (12 oz)	5–7 minutes	*Place* stalks towards outside of dish. *Reposition* during cooking.
Aubergine	450 g (1 lb) sliced	8–10 minutes	*Stir* or *shake* after 4 minutes.
Beans, broad	450 g (1 lb)	6–8 minutes	*Stir* or *shake* after 3 minutes and test after 5 minutes.
Beans, green	450 g (1 lb)	12–16 minutes	*Stir* or *shake* during cooking period. Time will vary with age and size.
Beetroot, whole	4 medium	14–16 minutes	*Pierce* skin with fork. *Reposition* during cooking.
Broccoli	450 g (1 lb)	10–12 minutes	*Reposition* during cooking. *Place* stalks towards outside of dish.

Vegetable	Quantity	Approximate time on HIGH setting	Microwave Cooking Technique(s)
Brussels sprouts	225 g (8 oz) 450 g (1 lb)	4–6 minutes 7–10 minutes	*Stir* or *shake* during cooking.
Cabbage	450 g (1 lb) quartered or shredded	9–12 minutes	*Stir* or *shake* during cooking.
Carrots	450 g (1 lb)	10–12 minutes	*Stir* or *shake* during cooking.
Cauliflower	whole 225 g (8 oz) florets 450 g (1 lb) florets	12–16 minutes 7–8 minutes 10–12 minutes	*Stir* or *shake* during cooking.
Celery	450 g (1 lb) sliced	7–10 minutes	*Stir* or *shake* during cooking.
Corn-on-the-cob	2	6–8 minutes	*Wrap* individually in greased greaseproof paper. *Do not* add water. *Turn* over after 3 minutes.
Courgettes	450 g (1 lb) sliced	8–12 minutes	*Do not* add more than 30 ml (2 tbsp) water. *Stir* or *shake* gently twice during cooking. *Stand* for 2 minutes before draining.
Fennel	450 g (1 lb) sliced	9–10 minutes	*Stir* or *shake* during cooking.
Leeks	450 g (1 lb) sliced	10–12 minutes	*Stir* or *shake* during cooking.
Mushrooms	225 g (8 oz)	2–3 minutes	*Do not* add water. Add 25 g (1 oz) butter and a squeeze of lemon juice. *Stir* or *shake* gently during cooking.
Onions	225 g (8 oz) sliced 175 g (6 oz) whole	4–6 minutes 10–12 minutes	*Stir* or *shake* sliced onions. *Add only* 60 ml (4 tbsp) water to whole onions. *Reposition* whole onions during cooking.
Parsnips	450 g (1 lb)	10–16 minutes	*Place* thinner parts towards centre. *Add* knob of butter and 15 ml (1 tbsp) lemon juice with 150 ml ($\frac{1}{4}$ pint) water. *Turn* dish during cooking and *reposition*.
Peas	450 g (1 lb)	9–11 minutes	*Stir* or *shake* during cooking.
Potatoes Baked jacket	1 × 175 g (6 oz) potato 2 × 175 g (6 oz) potatoes 4 × 175 g (6 oz) potatoes	4 minutes 6–8 minutes 12–14 minutes	*Wash* and prick skin with fork. *Place* on absorbent kitchen paper or napkin. When cooking more than 2 at a time, arrange in a circle. *Turn* over halfway through cooking.
Boiled (old)	450 g (1 lb)	7–10 minutes	*Stir* or *shake* during cooking.
Boiled (new)	450 g (1 lb)	6–8 minutes	*Do not* overcook or new potatoes become spongy.
Sweet	450 g (1 lb)	5 minutes	*Wash* and prick skin with fork. *Place* on absorbent kitchen paper. *Turn* over halfway through cooking time.
Spinach	450 g (1 lb)	6–7 minutes	*Do not* add water. Best cooked in roasting bag, sealed with non-metal fastening. *Turn* dish during cooking.
Swede/Turnip	450 g (1 lb) diced	10–15 minutes	*Stir* or *shake* during cooking.

I·N·D·E·X

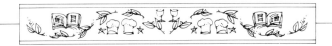